1085

GOODLY

HERITAGE

J. Paul Taylor

a Bishop of the
Free Methodist Church

Published by

Light and Life Press
Winona Lake, Indiana

PREFACE

The chapters of this book were originally delivered, for the most part, as addresses at ministers and superintendents conferences. They grew out of an abiding conviction that the present cannot be severed from the past without jeopardizing the future. The church has a family tree, and it would be as fatal to cut the tree down for fire-wood, as to sleep self-complacently in its shadow. Some ignore the past as if they were "the first that ever burst into this silent sea," and created something worth recording. While it might be an indication of religious madness to *dwell* among the tombs, an occasional *visit* to the cemetery of the past for a fresh glance at the monuments of heroes "who being dead yet speak," should stimulate to deep devotion and high endeavor.

The stream of spiritual religion, originating in primitive Christianity, flowed underground most of the time, through a thousand years. When Luther struck the dry rock the crystal waters burst forth anew, and a multitude heard the cry, "Ho, every one that thirsteth, come ye to the waters." Later when the stream had frozen into solid ice as a result of the frigid formality in the Established Church of England, Wesley prayed until the warm breath of the Spirit brought the springtime of revival, and the frozen streams melted into a flood of blessing that poured through all the channels of church and national life. Free Methodism fell heir to these benefits, although one hundred years ago she was disinherited as a daughter of Methodism so far as ecclesiastical privileges were concerned. The richer our inheritance the deeper in debt we are.

> *"They who on glorious ancestry enlarge*
> *Produce their debt instead of their discharge."*

This is the sole burden of these messages, and we trust it will be the great concern of the Free Methodist Church as she fronts her second century.

J. PAUL TAYLOR

Winona Lake, Indiana
January, 1960

CONTENTS

ACKNOWLEDGMENTS

Quotations in the first three addresses are largely from nineteenth century writers who had access to sources that put them in possession of a wide range of knowledge in the fields of ancient and medieval church history. For this material I am indebted largely to Ulhorn's *Conflict of Christianity with Heathenism,* and F. W. Farrar's *Early Days of Christianity.* Other works that have been helpful are Lord's *Beacon Lights of History,* Eusebius' *Ecclesiastical History,* T. R. Glover's *The Conflict of Religions in the Early Roman Empire,* Wm. M. Ramsay's *Church in the Roman Empire,* Westcott's essay on "The Two Empires; The Church and the World," in his work on *The Epistles of John,* and D'Aubigne's unsurpassed *History of the Reformation.* John Wesley's *Works* are largely drawn upon in the third address because Wesley is clearer than those who undertake to paraphrase or interpret him. Inspiration and suggestions for the fourth address came from many sources, including the following: Bishop Wilson T. Hogue's *History of the Free Methodist Church,* also his Semi-centennial sermon, *Retrospect and Prospect;* B. T. Roberts' *Why Another Sect;* Elias Bowen's *Origin of the Free Methodist Church;* B. H. Roberts' *Benjamin Titus Roberts;* bound copies of *The Earnest Christian;* and various booklets written a hundred years ago, on the issues that resulted in the founding of the Free Methodist Church.

Chapter 1

A HERITAGE FROM EARLY CHRISTIANITY

That we have arrived at a critical juncture in world history is admitted by all thoughtful persons. There is a ferment beneath the surface of society which with increasing frequency breaks through with explosive force. Gigantic movements are coming to grips with each other and contending for supremacy. Foundations are shaking, and the temple of civilization is tottering. And yet there is nothing unprecedented about the present crisis except the scale of it. The demons that now trouble and torment the human race have troubled and tormented it before, incarnated in slightly different forms. We are simply suffering from a fresh epidemic of an old disease, and some of its outbreaks in the past have been more virulent than the one we are now witnessing if not so widespread. The Church has been deeply involved in all the crises of the past because moral and spiritual elements have always been involved. A crisis is created by the breaking loose of the masses from moral and religious anchorage to sweep downward like an avalanche with ever accelerating momentum. At such times the church is called upon to challenge and check the descending movement. She can do this only as she possesses an adequate dynamic.

The New Testament Church was born in a crisis which in some respects has never been paralleled, and not only survived, but grew rapidly and mightily prevailed. The Roman Empire arose upon the wreck of the Republic in the same period the Christian Church appeared. The kingdom of

7

heaven and the kingdom of earth stood confronting each other. They were as fundamentally antagonistic to one another as fire and water. Conflict was inevitable. The forces pitted against each other were absurdly unequal from every material standpoint. Rome controlled the wealth of the world; the heralds of the cross were pitifully poor. Rome had her iron legions of fully armed men; the soldiers of the cross were insignificantly few and bore no carnal weapons. Rome boasted the highest culture the world has ever known, in some respects; in the van of the Church's march were a few ignorant and unlearned men with a liberally educated Pharisee who had espoused the new cause and abjured all wisdom of words lest the cross of Christ should be made of none effect. But their struggle was not with flesh and blood. Their assault was on the invisible government of the prince of this world.

Contemporary historians painted the picture in lurid colors. Visualize, if possible, the mountain of iniquity that this almost invisible grain of mustard seed called "the Church" essayed to overthrow. Striking counterparts of many features in the picture of that old Roman world stand out prominently in our twentieth century civilization.

The first step in the downward decline was the collapse of faith and reverence. Paul says of that pagan world, "They did not like to retain God in their knowledge." Long before Paul's day skeptical philosophies undermined faith in the old deities among the Greeks. On the stage the gods were made sport of in comedy. As the Greek culture and manners filtered into Rome, the Greek skepticism, like a "pestilence that walketh in darkness," filled the atmosphere. The literature of the time is strongly marked by a rationalistic spirit. When we read the subtle hypotheses pro-pounded by arrogant unbelievers 2,000 years ago, modern doubts and denials seem like nothing more than new duplicates of old negations and sophistries. Lucretius in his work on "The Nature of Things" contended that "in no wise the nature of all things for us was fashioned by a power divine." On the contrary, he holds that every object, (man included), is a peculiar conjunction and combination of atoms which will disintegrate and re-combine in other forms in an almost endless series, but there is no personal immortal-ity for man since the soul is mortal. "No man wakes up on whom once falls the icy pause of life," he says, and then proceeds to recommend suicide if life has come a burden and an offence. It sounds like an echo of Lucretius to hear a modern writer summarize much of modern thought in a poem, a few lines of which are as follows:

"Ages of earth are in me. I am made
Of time's immortal matter, which is dust.
I am old atoms in a new parade;
I am new iron miracled from rust.

"Where shall we go who came from conflagrations
Unkindled and unquenched within the Vast?
Oblivion is the home of destinations,
And darkness is our domicile at last."

The blank vacancy and hopelessness which ensued upon the loss of faith among the Romans is reflected in the words of Pliny, "There is nothing certain save that nothing is cer-tain, and there is no more wretched and yet arrogant being than man. The best thing which has been given to man amid the many torments of this life, is that he can take his own life." As erroneous as were the conceptions of Deity entertained by the Romans, their fear of the gods had a salutary, restraining influence on life. When atheism became prevalent and belief in a Divine government was lost, no fear of retribution remained to hold the worst propensities of men in leash. In the days of the Republic, Polybius said of the Romans, "Among them, the administration of public funds is more secure by means of the oath than elsewhere through the most extensive system of checks"; and in the early days of the empire, Plutarch said, "Sooner may a city exist without houses and ground, than a state without faith in the gods. This is the bond of union, the support of all legislation." When faith in its lowest form is lost by a people and there is no longer any fear of God before their eyes, then comes a general moral collapse, for the only foundation that can sustain good morals has been swept away. So it was in Rome. Let Seneca, the adviser of Nero, read the indictment. He says of his day, "All things are full of iniquity and vice. More crimes are committed than can be remedied by force. A monstrous contest of wickedness is carried on. Daily the lust of sin increases; daily the sense of shame diminishes. Casting away all regard for what is good and honorable, pleasure runs riot without restraint. Vice no longer hides itself, it stalks forth before all eyes. So public has iniquity become, so mightily does it flame up in all hearts, that innocence is no longer rare; it has ceased to exist." And somewhat later Lucian corroborates this indictment by exclaiming, "If any one loves wealth, and is dazed by gold; if any one measures happiness by purple and power; if any

10

one brought up among flatterers and slaves has never had a conception of liberty, frankness, and truth; if any one has wholly surrendered himself to pleasures, full tables, carousals, lewdness, sorcery, falsehood and deceit, let him go to Rome." Livy, the historian, sighs, "Rome has become great by her virtues till now, when we can neither bear our vices nor their remedies." Every department of life on all levels of society was shot through and through with the deadly virus of unspeakable depravity. Nothing remained to inspire conscientious living, for the very ideals and standards of life had become debased. The home, that great cornerstone of civilization has crumbled. Conjugal and filial affection were a curiosity. The man who contemplated matrimony was ridiculed, for little confidence in the ancient womanly virtues was felt. Rome, which for hundreds of years had not seen a divorce, had become so cursed by the common dissolution of the marriage ties, that Seneca could ask, "Does any woman now blush on account of divorce, since the time when certain distinguished women, of noble families, reckon their years not by the number of the annual consuls, but by that of their husbands? and go forth (from their husbands) for the sake of being married, are married for the sake of being divorced?" Matrimonial fidelity provoked mirth and contempt. Wily adventuresses as base as they were beautiful were held in high esteem.

Thousands of children were exposed to die of hunger or cold, or to be devoured by wild beasts, for childhood was not loved by adults. The aged were likewise exposed, for years were not honored or respected by youth. Innocent diversions and pleasures were *passe*. Gluttony and intemperance were indulged to almost unbelievable extremes. For-

11

tunes were spent on a single banquet. Pliny said that "A large part of mankind had come to think drunkenness the one prize of life, and to feel that the purpose for which they had been begotten was to drain vast draughts of stupefying wines from lascivious goblets." The theaters were the foulest incubators of vice, the performers being personally the most reckless and abandoned characters who were paid high salaries while public benefactors lived in want and neglect. The literature of the day reeked with filth, and that art was inspired and polluted by the touch of unclean spirits from the lowest hell is proved by productions of that day preserved under lava beds in Pompeii, from which many a traveler has turned away with a blush of deep revulsion. Half the population of Rome was made up of slaves and the other half lived in idleness and self-indulgence at the expense of the government. The people had abundance of leisure and the State provided entertainments for them that not only helped them to kill time but also helped them to kill their consciences. Such a government made few and feeble attempts to put a check on the most notorious iniquity. The vilest excesses, in which all uncleanness was worked with greediness, were so far from being condemned that they had the sanction of religious example, the temples being hotbeds of flagrant vice equal to the worst brothels, according to contemporary testimony.

When the sensibilities became so jaded and dulled that they were no longer excited by animal "pleasures seasoned high and tasting strong of guilt," resort was had to indescribable exhibitions of cruelty. Men could not be gratified by scenes being merely *played on the stage*. They must be *real events*. One actor was literally crucified on the stage and

12

mangled by a bear, and then flung himself down to cover the floor with blood. Another in his part of a play thrust his hand into a flame and stood motionless while it burned. Another was tossed and gored by a wild bull, while still another ascended a funeral pyre to be veritably burned alive. Dean F. W. Farrar comments, "It was the ultimate romance of a degraded and brutalized society. The Roman people 'victors once, now vile and base,' could now only be amused by sanguinary melodrama. Fables must be made realities, and the criminal must gracefully transform his supreme agonies into amusements for the multitude by becoming a gladiator or a tragedian." Then there were the wholesale slaughters in the gladiatorial shows, where in the presence of a throng that crowded the Colosseum, sometimes hundreds of men fought unto death with sharp weapons while the spectators howled their horrible delight. Sometimes the contest was between men and ravenous beasts. Friedlaender is quoted as saying that "the people were seized with an actual mania, in all ranks, of either sex, for these terrific and ghastly spectacles." To vary the frightfulness, sea battles were arranged, nineteen thousand men engaging on one occasion in desperate conflict for the amusement of the multitude that lined the shore.

When the cup of cruelty lost its power to intoxicate,

> "On that hard pagan world disgust
> And secret loathing fell;
> Deep weariness and sated lust
> Made human life a hell."

With the ability to enjoy present excitements dead, and

13

with no hope for the future, suicide seemed to offer a way of escape from a burned out life, and suicide became so common that no notice was taken of it. The whole situation might be summarized in the words of Dr. Lord, "A grinding and restless imperial despotism, a sensual and proud aristocracy, a debased and ignorant populace, enormously disproportionate conditions of fortune, slavery flourishing to a state unprecedented in the world's history, women the victims and the toys of men, lax sentiments of public and private morality, a whole people given over to demoralizing sports and spectacles, pleasure the master passion of the people, money the mainspring of society, a universal indulgence in all the vices which lead to violence and prepare the way for the total eclipse of the glory of man. There were no powerful conservative forces; the poison had descended to the extremities of the social system. A corrupt body must die when vitality has fled. The soul was gone; principle, patriotism, virtue had all passed away." This was Rome, not in a barbarian state but at the zenith of the best man-made civilization. No wonder that even Juvenal was appalled and despairingly said, "There will be nothing further which posterity may add to our evil manners; those coming after can only reproduce our desires and deeds. Every vice stands already at its topmost summit." If Juvenal were living today he would see the blackest spirits that haunted Rome in her worst days, issuing again from the pit, and history repeating itself. We leave it to you to trace the parallels line by line between the Roman civilization of the first centuries and the boasted civilization of these latter days.

We are interested in how the early Church invaded that decadent Roman world, and won her way through to an ultimate, permanent triumph. It was not an easy march to the goal of victory. The Church had the remedy needed by a morally diseased world; she had the bread needed by a spiritually starving world, but she came with a demand as well as a boon. Her principles and practices resisted the whole drift of sordid materialism and ungodliness. Her message called men to self-abasement and world renunciation. The world was not long in giving her answer in the form of violence and hate. Paul and his fellow laborers had encountered perils and persecutions in the first efforts at evangelism, but it was not until the later days of Nero that the Church as a body came into collision with the Imperial Government. Nero, the man who was called a "mixture of mud and blood" by those of his own day, and whom a modern writer has called "the epitome of the age in which he lived—the consummate flower of Pagan degradation," wreaked his fury upon the Christians after they were falsely accused of kindling the fires that reduced large sections of Rome to ashes. He had many of them sewed in the skins of wild beasts to be torn to pieces by ferocious dogs. He illuminated his gardens for night revels by having Christians covered with pitch and thus turned into human torches. Time does not suffice to tell the story of the prolonged periods of persecution which followed, with only short respites from danger and death, across three centuries. Many thousands of men, women, and children were subjected to unimaginable tortures. Some had the flesh torn from the body with iron pincers. Some had the members of the body gradually consumed by slow fires. Some were left to die of hunger and thirst in dark dungeons. Others were torn limb from limb by the power of horses pulling in opposite directions. Others were dragged by the feet over the rough cobblestones of the pavement until death liberated them. Many were brutally mutilated. Multitudes were thrown to the lions. Every instrument of torment that could be invented by diabolical ingenuity was used to defeat or exterminate the Church.

But she marched on to conquest through suffering. Tertullian declared, "The blood of martyrs is the seed of the church," and it was no idle boast when he said to the Romans, "We are of yesterday and yet have filled every place belonging to you—cities, islands, castles, towns, assemblies, your very camp, your tribes, companies, senate and forum; we leave to you your temples only." The Empire was covered with a network of Christian churches, and Constantine ultimately made Christianity the state religion because it had succeeded. The little lump of leaven had permeated the mass of meal. Such a phenomenon must be accounted for. Every effect must have an adequate cause. The cause that was sufficient then is sufficient now. What was the secret dynamic of that cause?

1. Those early Christians possessed an unclouded certainty as to the truth of the things to which they bore witness. The shadow of a question mark did not darken the brightness of their testimony. They spoke with no wavering voice. They did not mouth hypotheses; they did not venture guesses. They did not invest their all in an illusion. They had not followed cunningly devised fables. They were not victims of delusive dreams. Assurance is power; uncertainty is impotence. The tread is firm when one is sure of the path he is on and knows where he is going. The Christians who faced Rome could say, "We speak that we do know and

testify that we have seen." Their faith was "the substance of things hoped for, the evidence of things not seen." A halting or hesitant testimony would have betrayed the unreality of their experience and would have been wholly ineffective. Their declarations were bold because they had *found* the pearl of great price. They were sure of God because they lived in daily fellowship with Him. They were sure of Heaven because they possessed "the earnest of the inheritance." When Justin stood before the prefect Rusticus to be condemned to a martyr's death, he was asked, "Do you suppose that you will ascend up to heaven to receive some recompense there?" to which he readily replied, "I do not suppose, but I know it." The unreality of much modern religion is revealed in the language of hunger used by many professed Christians instead of the language of satisfaction. Their testimonies have the note of yearning and a suggestion of groping rather than of grasping and possessing. They talk about what they want to be and of what they are trying to be. It is not the exultant announcement of those who have arrived. Their desires are those of people reaching uncertainly after something not as yet found, whereas the desires of genuine believers are those of people who have entered the Kingdom of "righteousness and peace and joy in the Holy Ghost," and the taste they have experienced has aroused a craving for more. The members of the early Church had tasted and seen that the Lord is gracious and they went everywhere crying, "O taste and see that the Lord is good." Christ was the chief topic of their conversation. To every question asked of one by his persecutors the reply was, "I am a Christian." Like Paul, such persons were pressed in spirit and testified. As they mused upon the riches of

17

God's grace the fire burned, then spake they with their tongues. Evangelism was not confined to a class. Every believer was a herald. Every disciple was an apostle. Every child of God was an ambassador of Christ. Every member of the Church was a gospel propagandist. They had not learned the modern art of "becoming torpid in easy church hammocks while leaving spiritual work almost exclusively to ministers." They could not become torpid with the word of God like fire shut up in their bones. To them Christian work was not a "narcotic to spiritual doubt and emptiness." They had something to tell forth and the world stopped to listen as it always does when the note of unaffected reality is sounded.

2. The clear testimony of those early Christians was corroborated by the purity of their lives. Their outward deportment marched to the music of the professed inward experience. They consistently abstained from the vices universally indulged. They were not conformed to this world, but kept themselves unspotted from it, and the world thought it strange that they ran not with them to the same excess of riot. They abstained from all appearance of evil. They lived in a crooked and perverse generation without becoming crooked and perverse. They walked through an endless scene of pollution and kept their garments white. The leprosy of evil raged around them and they escaped the foul contagion. But theirs was more than a negative abstinence from the ways of the world. Their wholesale renunciations would have spelled bankruptcy to them had not the compensating gifts of grace divinely great and forever satisfying, been bestowed. It was the positive outshining and overflowing of superior values in the lives of Christians

that awakened unspeakable hunger in the pagan breast. If those primitive Christians forgot the artificial toys and joys of sense it was because they were evermore preoccupied with the unforgettable joy of the Lord. If they lightly valued wealth and estates it was because they were rich in faith and heirs of a kingdom that cannot be moved. If they looked with contempt upon place and power it was because of the princely dignity to which they had been exalted in heavenly places in Christ Jesus. If they had lost interest in "social figments, feints, and formalisms," it was because they had been charmed by the presence of One who is "fairer than the children of men." If they stayed far from the "banquetings and abominable idolatries" of the day it was because they had no time or taste for them since Christ had brought them into His banqueting house under the banner of love to sit down under His shadow with great delight and find His fruit sweet to the taste. If they left the "strifes for grassy garlands" to others it was because the crown of glory that fadeth not away was kept in sight. If they forsook the fashion parade and abjured decoration and display it was because they had received a better adorning. To the Christian women who had laid aside the gaudy attire of the world for Jesus' sake, Tertullian said, "Go forth, then, amply supplied with the cosmetics and ornaments of prophets and apostles, taking your dazzling whiteness from simplicity, and your ruddy hue from modesty; painting your eyes with bashfulness, and your mouths with silence; inserting in your ears the words of God and fastening on your necks the yoke of Christ. . . . Busy your hands with spinning, and keep your feet at home, and hand and foot will please more than if arrayed in gold. Clothe yourselves with the silk of upright-

19

ness, the fine linen of holiness, and the purple of modesty. Thus adorned you will have God for your lover." He might have added "and thus the world will be won." Arrayed in the beauties of holiness and decorated with the jewels of all lovely graces, these believers adorned the doctrine of Christ and gave it influence in the world by the attractions of holy living. They professed great things and they proved the profession true by the way they lived. It radiated from their faces. It sounded in the tone of their voices. It emerged in all their doings. The world marvelled, and millions obtained like precious faith and helped to swell the tide of world-redemption.

3. The unfailing love of those early Christians was one of the chief elements of their power. The ancient world was a world without love. Uhlhorn says, "Pagan antiquity was thoroughly egoistic . . . Every one sought his own interests regardless of others—self was the center around which everything revolved." Men wondered when they saw large areas of the desert waste rejoice and blossom as the rose because the flower of love, a celestial exotic, flourished perennially in a world of hate. Looking at the company of believers they exclaimed until it became a proverb, "Behold how they love one another." This new race of men addressed each other as brethren, and they lived as if they were members of one great family. They greeted one another with a holy kiss and it was no empty ceremony. They served one another. They condescended to one another. In honor they preferred one another. They prayed one for another. "They love each other without knowing each other," said an astonished pagan, and well might he be astonished in a world where Plautus declared, "A man is a wolf to a man

whom he does not know." They loved the depressed classes that were despised by their unchristian neighbors, the enslaved, the poor, the abandoned. They loved the souls of men until they were prepared to make any personal sacrifice to win them over to the faith, some selling themselves into slavery that they might bring the influence of the gospel to bear upon their master and his family and slaves. The less they were loved the more abundantly they loved. Where hatred abounded their love did much more abound. When the pestilence raged and the heathen fled, thrusting the sick and the half dead into the streets, the Christians remained like ministering angels among the dead and the dying to bless those who had cursed them, and some of them perished in their self-forgetting work of mercy. They did this immediately after the most bitter persecutions and while the sword of martyrdom was still unsheathed. Many died praying for their executioners, repeating the prayer of the first Christian martyr, "Lord lay not this sin to their charge." Such a love, always true to itself, is invincible. Such a love is power. Such a love wins the day in the first century or in the twentieth.

4. The unwavering courage and patience of the early Christians broke the power of hostility. They knew how to suffer and endure. If they had tried armed resistance they would have been crushed into extinction. But the world became weary of punishing and killing people who offered no resistance. These Christians were so far from feeling a dread of torture and death that they made no attempt to escape from their enemies. On the other hand, hundreds came forth and offered themselves a sacrifice to their malice. Their persecutors were shamed by the inoffensiveness and

meekness displayed by them. It was no cold Stoical stolidity which steeled itself against pain, but kind submission to the cruel hand of man and a calm committal of the spirit by faith into the hand of God, that melted the heart of stone in the Roman world. Here were men, women and children who could face any kind of death with a smile on the face and a song of praise on the lips. They considered the day of martyrdom the marriage day of the soul. The passive graces and virtues which bore the greatest appearance of helplessness, did more to break and subdue the pagan will than all things else.

To recapitulate, those early Christians were certain of their faith and certainty is power; they lived godly lives and godliness is power; they exhibited undying love and love is power; they maintained a calm unwavering patience and patience is power. That type of Christian sainthood will make a noticeable impact on our age and will level the walls of opposition.

To what quarter of the Christian world may we look for the production of the old dynamic? Through what channels will the power come for the creation of such saintliness of character as we have delineated? It is one of the most striking signs of the times in which we live that religious liberalism, through some of its most prominent spokesmen, is confessing that it has failed. The track pursued by the modernist has led him first into a tangled wilderness of doubt, and then into a barren desert of disillusionment. Occasionally an extreme liberal regains his sense of direction, if only for a moment, and discovers that he had mistaken sunset for sunrise, and that his boasted progress of thought was really a rapid retreat from the goodly heritage of the old faith. A man

who was generally recognized as the popular high priest of
modern religious liberalism, a few years since preached a
sermon from the text, "Ask for the old paths." He was
induced to preach the sermon, he tells us, as the result of an
interview with a young man who came to him and said, "I
am a modernist. I never could force my mind back into the
narrow molds of the old theology, but sometimes, especially
in crises, when one wants deep rootage the modernist soil
seems thin. There were power and depth in that old
fashioned Christianity which sometimes we modernists lack."
Among other things said by this prominent liberal in his
sermon, indicating his misgivings about the whole structure
he has spent his life in building, are these words, "We fair-
weather modernists had better salute those old time Christians. They did not blink the facts. Instead of lying to
themselves about the kind of universe this is, they achieved a
faith strong enough to rise above it, carry off a spiritual
victory in the face of it, and in the darkest hours that ever
fell on human history they lifted high an ancient song,
'Therefore will we not fear, though the earth be removed,
and though the mountains be carried into the midst of the
sea; though the waters thereof roar and be troubled, though
the mountains shake with the swelling thereof—the Lord
of Hosts is with us; the God of Jacob is our refuge.' " How
about modernism by way of contrast? The preacher proceeds to say, "We do not believe this, we do not believe
that. We have given up this incredible idea and that obso-
lete doctrine. So we pare down and dim out our faith
by negative abstractions until we have left only the ghostly
remainder of what was once a great religion. Then seeing
how few our positive convictions are and how little they

23

matter, we grow easy going about everybody else's convictions and end in a general mush of concession. Then a crisis falls upon the individual soul, upon the family, upon the world at large, where a religion that is going to amount to anything must have deep conviction in it, . . . 'The rain descended, and the floods came, and the winds blew, and beat upon that house; and it fell not, for it was founded upon a rock'—how much we need that." What a revelation in that admission!

The old dynamic will come through those who have kept the old faith. We have kept the sound doctrine of Methodism unadulterated. We have kept it while apostate churches sneered. We have come to the kingdom for such a time as this. The providential opportunity for the Free Methodist Church is now. We have the truth of which many liberals are now feeling the lack. The world needs our gospel. We should fear only one thing. There is danger that we will congratulate ourselves upon possessing the form of sound words and meantime lack the supernatural qualification for the effective propagation of the doctrine. The liberals have cut the wires at one point by a negation, at another point by a doubt, and at another point by ridicule, and of course the power cannot come through wires that are cut. We may have all of the wires up and keep them intact but the switch may not be turned on and the power will no more come through our wires than through the cut wires of the liberal. To change the figure, imagine a master organist sitting at the console of a great organ. He moves his fingers over the keys with perfect skill. He is following the printed notes without error. The keys are touched in proper sequence and with proper emphasis. But all of the motions are use- less, because no music is produced by them and no music is produced because there is no wind in the pipes. We may be well instructed in the theory of our faith. We may know how to present our doctrines in an orderly and systematic way. We may know just where the emphasis ought to be placed. But we may make no music and the world will pass by without turning aside to listen, because the breath of the eternal spirit is not in the pipes. We must have the rushing mighty wind of Pentecost if the heavenly harmonies are to go forth. There is more than enough dead orthodoxy in the world. The salt has lost its savor and it is cast out to be trodden under foot of men. We must have the power of the Spirit of Pentecost. When it is lacking we will engage in all sorts of fussy and frantic futilities in the energy of the flesh. Programs, techniques and methods will monopolize our precious time, and our labor will be in vain because it is not in the Lord. Machinery has a place but it is a poor substitute for the living force which makes it run. "Keep up the fire, and leave the generous flames to shape themselves."

The type of religion that raised a supernatural standard against the desolating flood of iniquity in the Roman Empire, and not only checked its rush, but also hurled it back until countless thousands on the verge of being drowned in destruction and perdition found salvation and security in Jesus Christ, will meet the crisis of our sorely perplexed world. Let us be sure we have it and then go out to spread it in the might of the Holy Ghost.

Chapter 2

A HERITAGE FROM THE REFORMATION

Through many years of strenuous toil, holy living, happy witnessing and unspeakable suffering, the early Christian church won its way to a commanding position in the world. But the hour of her triumph was the beginning of a millennium of tragedy. While the world frowned upon her she was safe; when the world smiled upon her she was in peril, for the smiles turned to caresses and courtship, eventuating in marriage, with the Emperor Constantine officiating at the wedding without benefit of divine blessing. The bride of Christ became the unlawful wife of Caesar because of unfaithfulness to her Lord. Losing her spiritual vision and power she hungered for temporal glory and rule. She exalted herself as Empress of the nations and more than once, to all intents and purposes, wrested the scepter of authority from the hands of a king and imperiously lorded it over him in the name of a religion that had become a mask. A fitting symbol of the ages of Romish temporal dominance is the historical picture of Henry IV, in the year 1077, standing barefoot in the snow for three days before Pope Hildebrand's palace, pleading for pardon, until the pope decided his humiliation was sufficient to indicate his abject submission to the papal power.

The long Arctic night that followed the eclipse of the Church's glory was not relieved but rather underscored by the glittering Aurora Borealis called the Renaissance. Its purely humanistic character resulted in brilliant degradation without a spiritual dawn. There were individual candles piercing the night, but in general, darkness was upon the face of the deep, and chaos, the first-born of darkness, was the prevailing order, or more properly, disorder. Things were out of place. The time was out of joint. The church was out of tune. It was a topsy-turvy world.

Deformation calls for reformation. There must be a movement of the Spirit in the darkness, on the face of the deep, to bring beauty out of deformity, order out of confusion, and harmony out of discord. Long before Luther there were forerunners of the Reformation. From time to time rumblings of discontent were heard and flashes from the crater of the volcano were seen, indicating fresh activity. But with the advent of Luther the volcano erupted and the earthquake of the Reformation shook the foundation and walls of an ecclesiasticism that was hoary with age and rotting with iniquity.

One hundred years before Luther, John Huss, "The John-Baptist of the Reformation," when driven out of Prague, said, prophetically, "The wicked have begun by preparing a treacherous snare for the goose (Huss signifying goose). But if even the goose, which is only a domestic bird, a peaceful animal, and whose flight is not very high in the air, has nevertheless broken through their toils, other birds, soaring more boldly toward the sky, will break through them with still greater force. Instead of a feeble goose, the truth will send forth eagles and keen-eyed vultures." Luther was the fearless eagle, of imperial character and mighty prowess, who defied and rode the tempest in triumph. *The Eagle* of Tennyson's fragmentary poem, to which we presumtuously add a verse, to fill out the picture, is a fitting symbol of

28

Luther, who, in turn, is a symbol of the Reformation.

"He clasps the crag with crooked hands
Close to the sun in lonely lands
Ringed with the azure world he stands.

"The wrinkled sea beneath him crawls
He watches from his mountain walls
And like a thunderbolt he falls."

He mounts aloft on tireless wings
To adore the glorious King of kings
And as he upward soars, he sings.

I. Take a clear look at Luther, the eagle of the Reformation, *standing* at the gates of the church. When, in the presence of the august dignitaries of church and state at the Diet of Worms, Luther gave utterance to the memorable words, "Here I *stand*. I can do no other. God help me," he was thinking of his firm, spiritual footing. He had found something that held him and bore him up, and upon which he could lay hold as Tennyson's eagle clasped the crag of the mountain with its powerful talons, without the slightest fear that the rock would crumble in their grasp. Two great certainties he possessed because they possessed *him*.

First, the supremacy of the objective revelation in the Scriptures, and second, the satisfaction of the subjective experience of justification by faith, witnessed to by the Holy Spirit. Luther seized the external and the internal realities of the faith and clung to them with unrelaxed tenacity. Like the great angel of the Apocalypse with one foot on the land

29

and the other on the sea, the Reformer stood with one foot on what Gladstone called "the impregnable rock of Holy Scripture," and the other on the unshakable rock of holy experience.

From the time he discovered the inspired Book, until his death, in all of his discussions, defenses, preaching and teaching, he made the Bible the first and last court of appeal. At Worms he challenged his opposers to convince him that he was wrong "through proofs from Holy Scripture." In his dispute with Doctor Eck, he said, "Our Doctor Eck has this day skimmed over Scripture almost without touching it—as a spider runs upon water. The reverend doctor flees from the Scriptures, as the devil from before the cross. As for me, with all due respect to the Fathers, I prefer the authority of Holy Writ." When Luther was offered the opportunity to defend his position before a church council he expressed his willingness to make his defense there if the Word of God would be recognized as final authority.

Luther protested against the elevation of the sacraments above the Word. He declared, "What is most precious in every sacrament, and consequently in the eucharist, is the promises and the Word of God. Without faith in these promises the sacrament is dead; it is a body without a soul, a cup without wine, a purse without money, a type without fulfillment, a letter without spirit, a casket without jewels, a scabbard without a sword."

Fundamentally it was the church and her pronouncements that had usurped the place of the Word. When the Augsburg Confession was read in the Palatine Chapel in the presence of state and church dignitaries, nine years after Luther made his stand at the Diet of Worms, the Bishop of

Wartzburg, referring to the church, exclaimed, "I stay with the mother, the mother, the mother." Brentz echoed the sentiments of Luther when he replied, "My Lord, pray do not for the mother forget either the Father or the Son." But that is precisely what the Romish church had done for centuries. The revelation of the Father and the Son, by the Spirit, in the Word, had been relegated to the limbo of almost forgotten things, and church traditions held sway. That is the perpetual position of Catholicism, and it must be met by the perpetual protest of all who believe the Bible. How completely the church of Rome undertakes to supersede the Word is evident in the confessions of one of her most eminent converts, John Henry Newman. Through many pages he details the religious opinions he held while in the Church of England, and then says, "From the time I became a Catholic, of course, I have no further history of my religious opinions to narrate . . . People say that the doctrine of Transubstantiation is difficult to believe; I did not believe the doctrine till I was a Catholic. I had no difficulty in believing it as soon as I believed that the Catholic Roman Church was the oracle of God, and that she had declared this doctrine to be part of the original revelation." Newman could not thus bow to the Church of Rome as the supreme authority without bowing the Bible out as the supreme authority. He held that the Bible was succumbing to the solvents that had made other authorities null and void with the passing of time.

Luther would have thundered in the ears of Newman as he did in the ears of Doctor Eck, "It is not in the power of the Roman pontiffs to make new articles of faith. The Christian believer acknowledges no other authority than

31

Holy Scripture. This alone is the *right Divine*. I beg the worthy doctor to concede that the Roman pontiffs were men, and that he will not make them gods."

Luther would never have been the spiritual Colossus he was, bestriding the world and shaking the nations, if he had not planted one foot on the granite of subjective reality in personal experience while the other stood solidly on the objective granite of the divine revelation in the Word. The personal experience of Luther parallels that of John Wesley in a remarkable way. Through minute devotion to duty, struggles unspeakable and fastings that brought him to the doors of death, Luther sought for peace. Staupitz, the vicar-general, and other leaders in the church attempted to help him. But it remained for an obscure, unnamed monk to quote some words of St. Bernard, as an unknown man quoted Luther in Aldersgate Street chapel two centuries later, and these were the words the monk quoted: "The testimony of the Holy Ghost in thy heart is this: Thy sins are forgiven thee." At once the day dawned and the day star arose in the heart of Luther, and with the light of assurance came the warmth of a new joy comparable to the strange warmth that pervaded Wesley's heart. Shortly thereafter, at the festival of Christmas, he took part in the worship of the day "with sweet emotion," and during the chanting of hymns, "his whole being responded *Amen*, and thrilled with joy."

Luther's experience discharged the priestly caste that posed as the heaven-appointed executor of the spiritual estate. The only assurance the supposed heir could have under the Roman system was the announcement by the priestly executor that the will was securely locked up in the vaults of the church. The whole transaction was taken care of by the ecclesiastics, and the only peace the supposed heir could have was the peace of presumption. Luther had the direct witness of the Spirit that he was a child of God, and being a child of God, he was an heir of God, and received the earnest of his inheritance in "righteousness and peace and joy in the Holy Ghost."

A church may boast "We have Luther to our father," but only those who follow the faith of Luther are the Reformation sons of Luther. Those who stand on the objective revelation alone or on the subjective experience alone are not true Protestants. Those who timidly and tentatively touch either side of spiritual reality will soon go out of balance and fall. The pendulum of Protestantism has swung from one extreme to the other. Some Protestants have no solid foundation in revealed historical facts. Others have no solid superstructure in assured personal experience. Many who rate themselves orthodox, survey the foundation in the Word and defend its divine origin with vigor, and sometimes, bitterness, but fail to rest on it as stones made living by regenerative grace. It is one of the strange anomalies of the religious realm that these persons, who make so much of the inspiration and authority of the Word, are so often rank Antinomians, lightly breaking the law of the Book they pretend to revere. They may profess to have become subjects of the new birth on the basis of credence given to the Bible statement that "Jesus Christ is the Son of God," without a heart faith answered by the witness of the Spirit, and it is no wonder that when the life belies the profession they resort again to the Scriptures to find justification for their sinning. The religious objectivists, at best, are unhappy legalists driven by themselves and dragged by others along the path of painful duty. They try to obey the law without having the law written in the heart. It is one of the tragedies of Protestantism that it embraces so many who wander all their days in the seventh chapter of Romans, buffeted between the walls of aspiration and defeat, groaning, "Who shall deliver me?" without finding the bright gate at the end of the long narrow cell, "I thank God through Jesus Christ our Lord," which opens out into the large place of Romans 8, with its life of liberty in the Spirit.

On the other hand are subjectivists who give almost exclusive attention to the superstructure, an air-castle religion, with no foundation except a foundation of mystical mist. They constitute a very large and comprehensive class including everything from the most extreme mystic to the most extreme liberal. On a winter day the fire was glowing in our fireplace. Turning suddenly to look out of the window, I was startled to see an evergreen shrub in the yard wrapped in flames. Almost immediately I realized that the window glass was reflecting the bright fire from the fireplace, upon the shrub. If a lingering doubt had possessed my mind about the unreality of the fire, it would have been dissolved by the obvious fact that while the flames glowed the shrub was crowned with cold snow. It was an attractive sight, but it presented a mere reflection of reality. And such is the subjective religion of multitudes who may hold very diverse religious opinions. Some glow in the presence of a rich ceremonial worship. It appeals to their aesthetic taste in precisely the same manner that a gorgeous scene or beautiful painting would appeal to it. Others are sentimentally tender over pathetic representations of the crucifixion who never

34

shed a tear of penitence over their sins for which Christ died. Still others lose themselves in mystical contemplation of the creations of their own imagination. Some resort to self-stimulation, or a species of self-hypnosis to rouse the feelings, "a sensuous mimicry of pious emotion," as John Caird called it. Many are charmed by the voice of the preacher when they do not propose to pattern their lives by his preaching. They have a long ancestry, for the Lord said to Ezekiel concerning his auditors, "Lo! thou art unto them as a very lovely song of one that hath a pleasant voice, and can play well on an instrument; for they hear thy words, but they do them not." Ezek. 33:32. A large company of subjectivists go on impressions and claim to be the recipients of special revelations that are utterly contrary to the teachings of the Word, and sometimes lead men into gross immorality and crime.

Those who like to be known as liberals have repudiated the Bible as God's supreme revelation to man, but are willing to admit the value of its ideals. The Bible may be a myth but it carries a useful message, they would say. But the ideal that has a mythical origin is as subjective and foundationless as the ideal that has a mystical origin. It is made of such stuff as dreams are made of, and exercises as little influence on character and conduct as the admiration for the human Jesus without adoration of the divine Christ had upon Rousseau, the brilliant libertine; Renan, the sentimental skeptic; and Napoleon, the scintillating general. The liberal is charmed by the picture of Jesus in the gospel history but is not changed by His personal presence in the heart. He is elated over mirages of a kingdom to come by human effort, but is not "translated into the kingdom of God's dear son" by the power of the Spirit, here and now.

35

In all these groups of subjectivists it is easy to discern the glow borrowed from the religion of Christ without its consuming fire. Men can become animated over a hundred things in religion, and at the same time be crowned with the cold snow of indifference or hostility to the ethical demands and the spiritual privileges of a holy faith. A religion of vivid imagination, keen sensibilities, warm emotions, fine aesthetic taste, lofty ideals, etc., leaves the heart a yawning void, for the objective reality of Christ revealed by the Book has not become a subjective reality by the appropriation of faith. Christ in history and Christ in heaven has not become Christ at home in the heart. Hence the play religion that leaves the inner man empty and unsatisfied. Spurgeon's characterization of such religion is too terribly true to be very humorous. He compares it to a man who calls his servant to prepare and serve dinner. The servant protests that he has nothing to set before him. But the master orders the table to be set. "And now," he says, "I will sit down to my meal, and you shall wait upon me. The empty dishes are brought in proper course; from invisible joints he cuts imperceptible slices, and from the empty plates he lifts upon his fork mouthfuls of nothingness and dainty morsels of vacuum." Then Spurgeon observes that when the "atmospheric banquet" was being consumed "its charms" would "require a very poetic and imaginative mind to appreciate them," and that the prospect of a second "unsubstantial feast" would be "somewhat undesirable and cheerless." This accounts for the multitude of church members who run madly after the scraps of pleasure offered by the world. They have an unreal religion in a world that seems to them very real. This unreal religion also accounts for the devastating effect upon many professors, of attacks by skeptical psychologists who attribute all religion to the fancies and hallucinations of disordered minds.

The old Methodists were the legitimate heirs of the Reformation for they sang with exultation and understanding,

> "What we have *heard* and *seen,*
>   With confidence we tell,
> And publish to the sons of men,
>   The signs infallible."

They *heard* the gospel history, and believed it as objective fact. They trusted the Christ of that history and could say, "He was *seen* of us also, as a subjective reality. We have not followed cunningly devised fables nor queerly conceived fantasies of our own minds, but were eye-witnesses of his majesty." This is the grace wherein we stand or we do not stand at all.

II. Take a long look at Luther, the eagle of the Reformation, *striking* at the gates of hell.

> "The wrinkled sea beneath him crawls
> He watches from his mountain walls
> And like a thunderbolt he falls."

And like a thunderbolt he strikes at the gates of hell, even though they have pictures of heaven painted on them. Dr. William R. Cannon said the Ninety-five Theses nailed on the door of the Wittenberg cathedral, by Luther, constituted "Protestantism's Declaration of Independence." And, may we add, it involved a declaration of war. Luther could not stand on the revelation in the Book and its duplicate in the breast without striking mighty blows against all that tended to subvert and destroy that revelation. And he was under no illusions as to the nature of the foe. It was not a case of Luther versus Leo, the pope; it was a case of Luther versus Lucifer. Men were but the tools and agents of Satan. Luther was affrighted neither by devils nor by dukes who were inspired by devils. When he was urgently advised by Spalatin and others not to go to Worms lest his life be in jeopardy, he answered that if they "should kindle a fire from Wittenberg to Worms that reached as high as heaven he would go through it in the name of the Lord, and would enter the jaws of this Behemoth, and break his teeth, confessing the Lord Jesus Christ." And, he said, "Even should there be as many devils in Worms as tiles on the housetops, still I would enter it." On his way he declared, "I will enter Worms under the banner of Christ against the gates of hell." On another occasion when he was told Duke George would oppose him, he let his informants know he would not be deterred "though it rained Duke Georges for nine days running."

At first Luther expected the pope to be the reformer of the church and the cleanser of the temple. In a letter to the pontiff he said, "It is true that I have attacked the court of Rome; but neither you nor any man on earth can deny that it is more corrupt than Sodom and Gomorrah; and that the impiety prevailing there is past all hope of cure. . . . The Church of Rome, once the foremost in sanctity, is become the most licentious den of robbers, the most shameless of all brothels, the kingdom of sin, of death, and of hell, which Antichrist himself, if he were to appear, could not increase in wickedness. All this is clearer than the sun at noonday. . . . It was for you and your cardinals to have applied the remedy; but the sick man mocks the physician, and the horse will not obey the rein. Rome deserves to have Satan himself for her king. So true it is that he reigns more than you in that Babylon."

Then the pope issued a bull anathematizing Luther and ordering his works to be burned. Luther commented, "At last I know that the pope is Antichrist, and that his throne is that of Satan himself." Then he publicly burned a copy of the bull, and the previous skirmishes issued in full scale war. When some counseled him to retract and make peace with the pope he replied, "This shall be my retraction: I said formerly that the pope was Christ's vicar; now I assert that he is our Lord's adversary, and the devil's apostle." Luther sounded forth the trumpet that never called retreat to the end of his life.

When he was criticized for the severity of his attacks against popery he answered, "Would that I could speak against it with a voice of thunder, and that each of my words was a thunderbolt!" It took this roughhewn, positive type of man to carry the battle to the enemy and sustain the on-slaught unflinchingly. The mild Melancthon, important as was his role in the Reformation, and the maneuvering Erasmus could never have led such a crusade. The critics of Luther's sharpness and roughness in recent times were answered conclusively by Alexander Maclaren in this lan-guage, "When a man is at death-grips with a tiger he may be pardoned if he strikes without considering whether he is going to spoil the skin or not; and that on the whole you cannot throttle snakes in graceful attitude. Men fought then (in Luther's day) with bludgeons; they fight now with dainty polished daggers, dipped in cold colorless poison of sarcasm. Perhaps there was less malice in the rougher old way than in the new."

A dedicated army of men with the courage and strength of Luther, if not with his ability, is desperately needed now, for Romanism still menaces the world. The principles and purposes of the Romish heirarchy are as changeless as gravity, although its procedures and plans may be as changeable as the wind. Its over-all strategy is the same as before the Reformation; its tactics adjust to the current situation. When Catholicism seems to double back on her track because of a political roadblock, she never loses sight of her ancient goal, namely, political domination.

Romanism had not changed when John Milton, in the first half of the seventeenth century compared it to a seductive Delilah, luring kings to sleep with heads pillowed on her lap while she robbed them of the powerful locks of law and then enslaved them until with recovered locks and restored power they pulled down the pillars of the temple of Dagon, and in one of his finest poems invoked the wrath of God on the "triple tyrant" who slaughtered the devout Piedmontese wholesale, and expresses the hope that others may escape "the Babylonian woe."

Romanism had not changed in the latter part of the same century when Jeremy Taylor, one of the great intellects of all time, in his *Dissuasive from Popery*, wrote a chapter with this heading, "The church of Rome, as it is at this day disordered, teaches doctrines, and uses practices, which are in themselves, or in their true and immediate consequences, direct impieties, and give warranty to a wicked life," and conclusively proved the truth of his charge.

It had not changed in France, at the same period of time, when Pascal, himself a Catholic, wrote his *Provincial Letters*, uncovering the inconceivable deceit and abysmal depravity of the Jesuits, whom Vinet called "Catholicism concentrated."

It had not changed in the beginning of the nineteenth century when Robert Southey, the poet laureate of England said, "Their system is as well the greatest work of human wisdom as it is of human wickedness," nor had it changed in the middle of the same century when William Morley Punshon, one of the most highly gifted ministers of English Methodism deplored "the corruption of Christianity by papal admixtures, blinding the world with the utter false-hood of half-truths, dazzling the senses and emasculating the understanding, trafficking in sin as in merchandise, and sell-ing escape from its penalties cheap."

It had not changed a little later when Spurgeon, possibly the most celebrated preacher of the last hundred years, said, "Popery is as much a masterpiece of Satan as the gospel is the masterpiece of God. There can scarcely be imagined any-thing of devilish craftiness or Satanic wickedness which could be compared with her; she is unparalleled, the queen of iniquity."

In the same era, Joseph Cook, the American scholar of scholars, lifted his mighty voice before one of the most cultured audiences in the land, warning that "the thin edge of the Romish wedge" was being "driven in with a muffled hammer," and reminding his auditors that in their day "One hundred and ninety millions of the human race are yet passing to and from through the snows of Canossa."

It is one of the most astounding and disturbing developments of our time, that in spite of its long history of cruelty and corruption, Romanism is having a strong resurgence. It succeeds because it is the religion of the natural man. When the English priest, Ronald Knox, remarked to Gilbert Chesterton that the Catholic Church would get on by hook or crook, and hastened to explain that he meant the fisherman's hook and the shepherd's crook, he suggested more than he suspected, for being in the boasted succession of Peter, Rome's fishermen are more interested in the coin in the fish's mouth than in the fish, and the fish is quite willing to yield up the coin for it helps pay his way to heaven, and her shepherds use the crook to herd into the ark of the church clean and unclean creatures without the slightest concern that they become new creatures. And if any of them are considered too bad for heaven and too good for hell they will be dropped off at purgatory and picked up later when they are pure enough for Paradise, providing their survivors can pay for their release. It is a religion ready-made for the sinner, which allows him to follow his depraved inclinations at will with the assurance that sufficient amends will be made by going to confession occasionally, attending mass, and trusting the priest who claims to hold the keys to the future world.

This is the religion that on the propaganda front is persuading many Americans that the only way to escape the whips of Communism is to expose themselves to the scorpions of Catholicism. Intelligent men are advocating gentle appeasement approaches from the Protestant side to resolve the differences between the two great branches of Christendom. Their naive suggestions remind one of the questions put to Job, "Canst thou draw out leviathan with an hook? or his tongue with a cord which thou lettest down? Will he make a covenant with thee? Wilt thou play with him as with a bird? or wilt thou bind him for thy maidens?" When the approach is from the Romanist side we are reminded of the episode in English history, in the days of Edward the Sixth, when the lord protector led a mighty army into Scotland to demand that their young queen Mary be given to King Edward in marriage. The Scotch, refusing to accede to the demand, were beaten by the English in battle. When the English asked a Scottish lord, who was taken prisoner in the battle, "Now, sir, how do you like our king's marriage with your queen?" he replied, "I always did like the marriage, but I do not like the wooing, that you should fetch a bride with fire and sword." We do not like Romanism's wooing by fire and sword in the past, nor her present wooing under false pretenses as exemplified in the syndicated articles published by a well-known Catholic organization and scattered across America in newspapers and magazines. And we do not like the proposed wedding, which would be a re-marriage after a separation that took place four hundred years ago, on the basis of a divorce secured on Bible grounds with Martin Luther, inspired by the Holy Spirit, pleading the case. In spite of the more than half-blind matchmakers in Protestantism who are promoting the courtship and recommending the union, every true Protestant will oppose it to the death, for he knows how softly Rome can purr where she does not have the upper hand, and how cruelly she can claw where she is in the ascendancy. A little spiritual discernment can detect the mixture of elements in Romanism as strange as the ingredients of the witches' brew in

Macbeth, and as morally confusing as the witches' chant, "Fair is foul and foul is fair." There can be nothing but a feeling of revulsion in a pure Protestant heart to proposals that we wed a religion that is a mongrel product of a previous wedding with paganism centuries ago. Such a heart would fully endorse the position taken by one of Mrs. Browning's poetical characters in speaking to another,

> *"I disbelieve in Christian-pagans, much*
> *As you in woman-fishes."*

While we are relentlessly opposing this unholy institution that forges the name "holy" on all its credentials, although it is an incubator of every kind of evil, we must not forget that the gates of hell open into many other areas of society. It is the business of Protestantism to protest against iniquity wherever it raises its head, whether the head wear a cowl or a crown or an ordinary cap, and back up its protest, not with the civil sword but with the sword of the Spirit. In our day of soft living there is a demand for soft preaching and if the preacher yields to the temptation to "smooth down the rough text to ears polite," his sermons will degenerate into delightful essays and "intellectual feasts," with everyone pleased with the preacher and with himself. Preaching should be searching and disturbing to those who are in rebellion against God. It should challenge and assault every stronghold of Satan. The severest truth can be spoken in love. The faithful messenger batters at the walls of the world's palaces because he knows the fancied palaces to be, in reality, prisons. He would demolish the prison because he hates it; deliver the prisoner because he loves him. If the

prisoner, under the intoxicating spell of the prince of this
world, fancies he is living in a paradise of pleasure and that
his chains are ornaments, he may consider the man who
tries to rescue him a rude kill-joy, but the true preacher in
the Protestant succession will continue to batter at the walls,
appealing from Philip drunk to Philip sober, knowing that
he will have the everlasting love and gratitude of the
imprisoned prodigal once he comes to himself and walks out
into the new life of liberty in Christ.

III. Take a fascinated look at Luther, the eagle of the
Reformation, singing at the gates of heaven.

> He mounts aloft on tireless wings,
> To adore the glorious King of kings,
> And as he upward soars, he sings.

Luther had discovered the long forgotten truth of the
priesthood of all believers, and now, not as a lone eagle,
but with a great flock of eagles that had broken out of
their cages in the Reformation, he mounted to the gates
of heaven to hold communion with God the father of all.
In the blazing light of God's countenance the distinction
between clergy and laity was lost. For organizational effi-
ciency some men are placed in positions of leadership, but
leadership does not mean the right to lordship over God's
heritage. In the spiritual realm the preacher and the layman
are on a par, because both are on the plane of a common
"royal priesthood" where questions of precedence, protocol
and superiority are irrelevant. When the layman and the
preacher mount up with wings as eagles and sit at the table
of God, they eat the same spiritual meat and drink the same
spiritual wine.

"There is a scene where spirits blend,
  Where friend holds fellowship with friend.
Though sundered far (in official respects) by faith they meet,
  Around one common mercy seat."

and all feel the same throb of joy in communion with heaven.

The joy must have an outlet. It must become articulate. No one can drink of the rivers of God's pleasures without having rivers of living water flow out of his innermost being, all of them shining and singing from fulness of joy. The Reformation brought the glad tidings of redemption. The year of jubilee had come and it was ushered in with a burst of holy song. A hundred years ago Henry Allon said, "The great principle of the Reformation was to restore the sense of personal as distinguished from vicarious religion. It was, therefore, a first inculcation that the people were to sing and to pray for themselves, and not the priests for them. Instead of drowsy monks droning out Latin Litanies which they themselves could not always construe, 'young men and maidens, old men and children,' with loud and rapturous voice, sang their vernacular praises to God. The morning was breaking, and it was hailed with joyous song." F. W. Krummacher, the noted German preacher wrote, "Among the noblest and loveliest of the results of the Reformation is the harvest of holy song. . . . The church for half a thousand years had been doomed to silence. She indeed had been permitted to add to the priestly litanies sung in unknown Latin, her 'Lord have mercy,' or her 'Amen,' but these had come to be mere soulless echoes. How happy was she made when her tongue was at last unloosed; when in church and at home she could utter, according to her heart's desire and longing, her Christian faith, renewed in apostolical purity, in the winged words of her own mother tongue!" Her hymnology "soared on eagle's wings in the most sublime and inspired lyrics."

Luther wrote many of the hymns of the Reformation, and Paul Gerhardt, one of the early sons of the Reformation, poured out an irrepressible flood of Christian poetry and melody. After a walk on a spring day, Gerhardt wrote,

> "The lark floats high before the breeze,
> The dove toward the forest-trees
>   From covert speeds along;
> The song encircled nightingale,
> In ecstasy, fills hill and dale
>   And mount and plain with song.
>
> "And shall I, can I, dumb remain?
> No, every power shall sing again
>   To God who loves us best.
> Come, let me sing! All nature sings,
> And all within me tribute brings
>   Streaming from out my breast."

Why should not Gerhardt and others sing? It was the time of a new vernal equinox in the kingdom of God. The church was hearing the voice of her beloved Bridegroom calling, "Rise up, my love, my fair one, and come away. For, lo, the winter is past, the rain is over and gone; The flowers appear on the earth; the time of the singing of birds is come, and the voice of the turtledove is heard in our land." The songs "streaming from out the breast" of Gerhardt flowed with vast volume down the years until John Wesley refreshed

47

his soul in their flow, and, translating many of them into the English language to run in the channels of Methodism, mingled them with the mighty current of Wesleyan hymnody. Blissful song was one of the chief sources of power in the Wesleyan revival as it was in the Reformation.

Dr. R. W. Dale, the noted Congregational preacher delivered a message in City Road Chapel, London, on March 4th, 1891, in connection with the observance of the centenary of John Wesley's death. In this message he said, "In the religious life of the early Methodists there was exhilaration, vigour, triumph. Their joy was irrepressible. It broke out in shouts of Hallelujah! It sang exulting songs. . . . Nor was it on Sunday only when engaged in religious services, that the Methodists had this abounding joy; it remained with them all the week through; there was a light resting upon their common path; their hearts were filled with music when there was no song on their lips. And so weary men and men who had been discouraged and broken down by trouble; and men who had come to despair of themselves because they had been defeated in every attempt to live a better life; and men who were miserable because they hated and despised themselves for their vices, and knew that others hated and despised them, too; and men who had become lethargic and dull because their horizons were narrow and their occupations and thoughts monotonous—men whose imaginations had never been kindled, whose hearts had never been stirred; and men who were happy as yet, but who had begun to see that the streams of earthly happiness soon run dry; all sorts of men where charmed, excited, by the discovery that people like themselves had found the springs of an immortal gladness and strength."

We are living in a day when many of the boughs on which men have built their nests are giving way because they are weak from rottenness and the poor songs of their occupants are cheerless. But those whose citizenship is in heaven,

> "Like the bird who pausing in her flight,
> Awhile on boughs too slight,
> Feels them give way beneath her, and yet sings,
> Knowing that she hath wings,"

far from being shaken because things here below are shaken or even shattered, mount above it all and "rejoice with joy unspeakable and full of glory." These are the ones who demonstrate the superiority of Christian realities to all the world offers. The people who can wing their way to heaven for communion with God, can sing their way through the world, and many disillusioned dupes of earth will be charmed and constrained to follow in their train. When the stream of holy song ceases, it will be because the fountain of holy joy has failed, and that will not happen while the holy life imparted by the Holy Spirit pulsates in human hearts. The roll of divine melody and harmony will never end, for there are many who will give it vocal expression until it blends with the song of Moses and the Lamb on high. Everyone may have a permanent place in the chorus that will sound forth the praises of God in time and eternity. This is a part of our heritage in the Reformation and in the Christ who made the Reformation possible.

The perils of the past have been met and mastered, and the perils of the present may be met and mastered by the humblest human instruments in the hands of God.

"O Truth! O Freedom! how are ye still born
  In the rude stable, in the manger nurst!
What humble hands unbar those gates of morn
  Through which the splendors of the New Day burst!

What! shall one monk, scarce known beyond his cell,
Front Rome's far-reaching bolts, and scorn her frown?
Brave Luther answered Yes; that thunder's swell
  Rocked Europe, and discharmed the triple crown."
                                        James Russell Lowell

Giant evils still stalk the earth, vaunting themselves, and threatening destruction to the Israel of God. But the God of Israel can yet make the weak things of the world confound the things that are mighty. Everywhere he is looking for a stripling with a sling and a stone and a boundless faith in the almightiness of his God. Such warriors will fell the giant for "the battle is the Lord's."

Chapter 3

A HERITAGE FROM EARLY METHODISM

In the middle of the eighteenth century a religious movement began in the Established Church of England, which, as has been said, "with the rapidity of a revolution, and the renovating power of a celestial springtime, passed over the United Kingdom and its dependencies." That movement has been variously appraised by friend and foe. To the one it was a spiritual revolution that prevented a political revolution. To the other it was a fanatical upheaval working endless havoc in the church. To the one it was a saving salt. To the other it was a disturbing leaven. The man who was the chief Founder and Director of the movement while swept along on its mighty current, had the amazing power to gauge something of its magnitude. In musical poetry he said,

"O the fathomless love that hath deigned to approve
   And prosper the work of my hands.
With my pastoral crook I went over the brook,
   And, behold, I am spread into bands.

"Who, I ask in amaze, hath gotten me these?
   And enquire from what quarter they came;
My full heart replies, 'They are born from the skies';
   And gives glory to God and the Lamb."

Then in plain prose he wrote, "The revival of religion has spread to such a degree as neither we nor our fathers had known. How *extensive* has it been! There is scarce a considerable town in the kingdom where some have not been made witnesses of it. It has spread to every age and sex, to most orders and degrees of men, and even to abundance of those who, in time past, were accounted monsters of wickedness. Consider the *swiftness* as well as the extent of it. In what age has such a number of sinners been recovered, in so short a time from the error of their ways? When has true religion, I will not say since the Reformation, but since the time of Constantine the Great, made so large a progress in any nation, within so small a space? I believe hardly can ancient or modern history afford a parallel instance. We may likewise observe the *depth* of the work so extensively and swiftly wrought. Multitudes have been thoroughly convinced of sin; and shortly after, so filled with joy and love, that whether they were in the body, or out of the body, they could hardly tell; and in the power of this love they have trampled under foot whatever the world counts either terrible or desirable, having evidenced in the severest trials an invariable and tender good will to mankind and all the fruits of holiness. Now so deep a repentance, so strong a faith, so fervent a love, so unblemished a holiness wrought in so many persons in so short a time the world has not seen for ages." *Sermons*, Vol. I, p. 495. So said John Wesley in poetry and prose.

Now such a phenomenon must be accounted for. Methodism is not a sporadic thing. It is not an emotional flash-in-the-pan. It is too deep and permanent to be that. It has been marked through the years by certain qualities and characteristics. Those qualities and characteristics belong essentially to moral and spiritual personality, fully redeemed. Dr. W. E. Sangster in his *Methodism Can Be Born Again*, poses this question as a chapter caption, "Is Methodism a Machine or a Message?" and answers that Methodism is a message. But it should be said, and Dr. Sangster would not contradict it, that Methodism is fundamentally a Man. Methodism must have machinery. (It was very simple at first.) But machinery does not run itself. The fuel of the machine is the message of Methodism. But a man puts the fuel in and guides the machine. Fundamentally a spiritual movement does not move on wheels but on feet, the feet of spiritual men. Methodism is not an abstraction, but a very concrete, personal thing. Methodism began with a man, John Wesley. It was a case in which a man came into possession of a lost secret, a treasure that had long been buried in the field of the church, undiscovered, because the plowing had been too shallow. It was a new edition, in a living, personal epistle, of the original New Testament religion, which had been out of print or sadly blurred for generations. A great historian said Wesley "was the embodiment of the movement" called Methodism. Wesley was Methodism condensed. Methodism is Wesley expanded. So we propose to consider Methodism not in terms of ecclesiastical polity but in terms of moral and spiritual personality.

Mrs. Pendarves, the young widow in whom Wesley took a romantic interest in his Oxford days named him "Primitive Christianity" in a letter to a friend. The appellation would have been a fitting one after the Aldersgate experience. In Wesley's own "Character of a Methodist" the prominent feature is conformity to the first and greatest commandment, which is both law and gospel. Although Wesley wrote under the title, "Not as though I had already attained," in the introduction he said, "Perhaps some of you who hate what

53

I am *called* may love what *I am* by the grace of God." His portrait of a Methodist is a portrait of himself, and Methodism is the portrait enlarged. Wesley's life text constantly repeated in his writings was the first and greatest commandment.

1. The process begins at the heart. "Thou shalt love the Lord thy God with all thy heart." The first throb of spiritual life always begins at the heart. John Wesley had trodden the weary rounds of a Protestant purgatory for years in search of the peace that assurance of pardon and sonship gives. Under the instruction of Peter Bohler he says, "I well saw, no one could have a sense of forgiveness and not feel it. I felt it not." Then on Wednesday evening, May 24th, 1738, he went to the meeting of a society in Aldersgate Street and an unnamed man arose and read Luther's preface to his commentary on Romans. While the Reformer's description of the change which God works in the heart through faith in Christ was being read, Wesley declared, "I *felt* my heart strangely warmed. I *felt* I did trust in Christ, Christ alone, for salvation; and an assurance was given me, that he had taken away *my* sins, even *mine*, and saved *me* from the law of sin and death. . . . I then testified openly to all there what I now first *felt* in *my* heart." Three sentences of testimony and in each sentence the word *felt* is used. Methodism is Methodism only as she believes in a heart-felt religion. Feeling in religion may be decried by the cold intellectuals of our day but the only way one may be sure of his relation to God is to have an assurance divinely given, and that assurance is accompanied by a deep heart feeling which is infinitely finer and richer than animal excitement. An American missionary asked a celebrated

54

European theologian what he considered the seat of final authority and certainty in religion. The theologian placed his left hand on the missionary's shoulder, and with his right hand smote his own breast as he replied, "Here, where the Jesus of history meets the Christ of experience. When steel strikes stone then come the stars." The man who is true to his reason is driven to believe there must be a personal, almighty God behind and within the universe. His footsteps and fingerprints are visible in the world. But by no rational process can a man arrive at any final satisfaction about the nature and purposes of this personal God. How he feels toward us, and what he desires to do for us must be revealed to the inner man. The day must dawn and the day star arise in the heart. Lord Alfred Tennyson went out in search of God. He desired to know him in personl intimate fellowship. This is the result,

> "I found him not in world or sun,
>   In eagle's wing or insect's eye,
> Nor through the questions men may try,
>   The petty cobwebs we have spun.

> "If e'er when faith had fallen asleep,
>   I heard a voice 'Believe no more,'
> And heard an ever-breaking shore,
>   That tumbled in the godless deep,

> "A warmth within the breast would melt,
>   The freezing reason's colder part,
> And like a man in wrath, the heart,
>   Stood up and answered, I have felt."

This "warmth within the breast" of John Wesley clarified his theology, and that involved correction of his religious grammar. That immediate, conscious, personal experience gave him a grammar of grace from that time forth, in which the first person, singular number, present tense, indicative mood predominated. Previous to Aldersgate, Wesley had droned in monotonous monotone with other churchmen, the collective confessions and petitions of the Established Church, punctuated by sighs for the unattained, and to them the unattainable because of their lack of faith. After Aldersgate it was no longer a hopeless cry in unison, that God would "cleanse the thoughts of our hearts by the inspiration of the Holy Spirit," but it was the individual Wesley and other individuals who had learned the secret of faith, and cried in exultation, "He does it! He does it for me! He does it now!" The ideal was clear to Wesley's penetrating intellect long before it became an inward reality. He preached his sermon on the "Circumcision of the Heart" before Oxford University in 1833, five years before he received the heart-warming experience, and the sermon is in the volume of his discourses which constitutes an important part of the doctrinal standards of Methodism. In the light of God's subsequent revelation to him he corrected, in an inserted paragraph, the spiritual grammar of the discourse to focus upon the individual in a presentation of gracious, present privilege. When Wesley went on his mission to the Indians in Georgia, Mr. Spangenberg, a Moravian pastor, asked him, "Have you the witness within yourself? Does the Spirit of God bear witness with your spirit that you are a child of God?" Noticing Wesley's surprise, he pressed him further with the question, "Do you know Jesus Christ?" and got the reply, "I know He is the Saviour of the world." "True," rejoined the pastor, "but do you know He has saved you?" and Wesley answered, "I hope He has died for me." Then Spangenberg asked, "Do you know yourself?" and Wesley answered, "I do." "But," he adds later, "I fear they were vain words." But the vain words became words of ringing certainty when the Son of God was revealed in him.

"Faith, Hope and Love were questioned what they
       thought
Of future glory which religion taught.
Now Faith *believed it*, firmly to be true,
And Hope *expected* so to find it too;
Love answered, smiling with a conscious glow,
'Believe! Expect! I *know* it to be so!'"

So wrote Wesley thirty-five years after Aldersgate. The "conscious glow" remained. Methodism is Methodism only as she has this "conscious glow."

2. A "love divine all loves excelling," which not only touches but also fills and possesses the heart, cannot leave the intellect unaffected. "Thou shalt love the Lord thy God with all thy mind" is an important part of the great commandment. Methodism from the beginning was accused of being an irrational movement controlled by uncontrolled impulses. Wesley, the embodiment of the movement, was a living contradiction of this. He had a highly trained mind. In his Oxford days he was recognized as a logician of first rank. The heart-warming experience did not smother his logical powers, but the warmth within his breast did melt the freezing reason's colder part, and made the mind of Wesley

57

not the least of his contributions to the church. He said to his followers, "You are in danger of enthusiasm every hour— if you lightly esteem reason, knowledge, or human learning; every one of which is an excellent gift of God, and may serve the noblest purposes. I advise you, never to use the words, wisdom, reason, or knowledge by way of reproach. On the contrary, pray that you yourself may abound in them more and more. If you mean worldly wisdom, useless knowledge, false reasoning, say so; and throw away the chaff, but not the wheat." Wesley was a lifelong student. He enriched his own mind constantly by reading, and provided a Library of Christian works for his Societies, which it was the business of every one of his preachers to circulate.

He knew both the power and the limitations of intellect. He did not open his mouth and shut his eyes to see what the Lord would give him. He opened the eyes of his mind but he knew there was a region beyond the range of reason. So he neither decried nor defied intellect. When he had tried unsuccessfully to persuade Bishop Lowth to ordain a preacher who knew no Greek or Latin, to go to America, he said, "Your Lordship *did* see good to ordain, and send into America, other persons who knew something of Greek and Latin, but who knew no more of saving souls than of catching whales," and then remarked as a wise guard to his words, "My Lord, I do by no means despise learning; I know the value of it too well. But what is this, particularly in a Christian minister, compared to piety? What is it in a man that has no religion? 'As a jewel in a swine's snout.' "

Wesley's intellect was the practical, organizing intellect, and the mark of practicality was on everything he said and did. Macauley gave him credit for having "a genius for

58

government not inferior to that of Richelieu," while Leslie Stephen declared, "his talent for business and for spiritual influence command equally our wonder." He was quick to see and seize the most fitting means to reach the highest ends. Although at first he thought it almost a sin to attempt to get a man converted outside the walls of the church, when he saw how the multitudes were reached by unconventional field preaching, his common sense led him to lift up his voice wherever men would hear. His class-meeting system was one of the wisest expedients ever adopted for Christian fellowship and edification. His choice of lay-preachers reveals a wisdom beyond that possessed by all the Church leaders of his time. His insistence on plain, simple preaching shows how correctly he gauged the needs of the masses.

Wesley's intellect was severely scientific. It was by the inductive method that he verified the conclusions at which he had arrived by a thorough study of the Scriptures. He questioned thousands of the subjects of grace, and carefully collated their testimonies. He knew that people in various places with different backgrounds, and different degrees of culture, giving like testimonies could not be in collusion, and all of them could not be wrong.

His mind demanded the pragmatic test in the presence of any profession of ministerial authority. One of the most remarkable documents from the pen of Wesley is a long letter written to two different clergymen at widely separated times, in which he contrasts a physician who has no legal authority to practise medicine and yet effects cures, with one who is legally authorized to practise but effects no cures, and by analogy contrasts his lay preachers who never had the authority of ordination and yet saved souls, with the ordained ministers of the church, who saved no souls. His conclusion is, "He is not a physician who effects no cures," and "he that saves no souls is no minister of Christ." To one who criticized his irregular preachers, he answered again with the pragmatic test, "A few irregular men openly witness those truths of God which the regular clergy (a few excepted) either suppress or wholly deny. Their word is accompanied with the power of God, convincing and converting sinners. The word of those is not accompanied with power; it neither wounds nor heals." No wonder he said at another time, "Soul-damning clergy lay me under more difficulties than soul-saving laymen."

Wesley had the philosophical intellect. He saw life whole. He knew how to harmonize contrasting facts. His balanced mind gave out a balanced ministry of complementary truths. He had the skill rightly to divide the word of truth and give each person his portion of meat in due season. He asks the question, "What is the means, as of begetting spiritual life where it is not, so of sustaining and increasing it where it is?" and answers, "Some think, preaching the law only; others, preaching the gospel only. I think neither the one nor the other; but duly mixing both, in every place, if not in every sermon. . . . I think the right method of preaching is this: at our first beginning to preach at any place, after a general declaration of the love of God to sinners, and his willingness that they should be saved, to preach the law, in the strongest, the closest, the most searching manner possible; only intermixing the gospel here and there, and showing it, as it were, afar off. After more and more persons are convinced of sin, we may mix more and more of the gospel, in order to beget faith, to raise into spiritual life those whom the law hath slain; but this is not to be done too hastily neither. Therefore, it is not expedient wholly to omit the law; not only because we may well suppose that many of our hearers are still unconvinced; but because otherwise there is danger, that many who are convinced will heal their own wounds slightly; therefore, it is only in private converse with a thoroughly convinced sinner, that we should preach nothing but the gospel. If indeed, we could suppose a whole congregation to be thus convinced, we should need to preach only the gospel: and the same we might do, if our whole congregation were supposed to be newly justified. But when these grow in grace, and in the knowledge of Christ, a wise builder would preach the law to them again; only taking particular care to place every part of it in a Gospel light, as not a command but a privilege also, as a branch of the glorious liberty of the sons of God. He would take equal care to remind them, that this is not the cause, but the fruit of their acceptance with God; that other cause 'other foundation can no man lay, than that which is laid, even Jesus Christ;' that we are still forgiven and accepted only for the sake of what he hath done and suffered for us; and that all true obedience springs from love to him, grounded on his first loving us. He would labour, therefore, in preaching any part of the law, to keep the love of Christ continually before their eyes; that thence they might draw fresh life, vigor, and strength, to run the way of his commandments. Thus would he preach the law even to those who were pressing on to the mark. But to those who were careless, or drawing back, he would preach it in another manner, nearly as he did before they were convinced of sin.

To those meanwhile, who were earnest but feeble-minded, he

would preach the gospel chiefly; yet variously intermixing more or less of the law, according to their various necessities." We give this lengthy quotation as a remarkable evidence that Wesley was a master in the art of spiritual dietetics. He had the skill to prepare and present a balanced menu.

He also had the wisdom to distinguish the divine element in the great revival from the other-than-divine elements that obtruded themselves upon the scene. To those who criticized the "fits" into which some of his followers were thrown under the movement of the Spirit, he frankly admitted that some of these exercises were human or perchance something worse since the devil would ape the work of God. But Wesley always refused to throw the gold out with the dross. He did not undertake to "sterilize fanaticism at the cost of extinguishing faith," to use Mr. Toynbee's language. On one occasion he wrote to his brother Charles, "This week I have begun to speak my mind concerning five or six honest enthusiasts. But I move only a hair's-breadth at a time; and by this means we come nearer and nearer to each other. No sharpness will profit. There is need of a lady's hand as well as a lion's heart." He could also see the danger of a drift to the opposite extreme. He knew that the fever of fanaticism is frequently succeeded by the chills of formalism. He followed the golden mean and prescribed such remedies for his patients as would bring them into spiritual health with its normal temperature. Writing to one of his revivalists, he said, "I sincerely wish you may retain your former zeal for God, only that it may be a 'zeal according to knowledge'! But there certainly will be a danger of your sinking into a careless, lukewarm state without zeal or spirit at all. As you were surfeited with an irrational, unscriptural religion, you may easily slide into no religion at all, or into a dead form that will never make you happy either in this world or in that which is to come." To Dr. Adam Clarke he wrote, "You will have need of all the courage and prudence which God has given you. Indeed you will want constant supplies of both. Very gently and very steadily you should proceed between the rocks on either hand. In the great revival of London my first difficulty was to bring to temper those who opposed the work, and my next to check and regulate the extravagances of those that promote it. And this was far the hardest part of the work, for many of them would bear no check at all. But I followed one rule, though with all calmness; 'You must either bend or break.' Meantime, while you act exactly right, except to be blamed by both sides." It always has been a good evidence that a man is walking in the middle of the solid road when he is being pelted with mud by the fanatics in the ditch on the right side of the road and by the formalists in the ditch on the left side of the road.

On all questions pertaining to church order Wesley always kept on an even keel. On one such question he remarked, "Here is Charles Perronet raving 'because his friends have given up all'; and Charles Wesley, 'because they have given up nothing'; and I in the midst, staring and wondering both at the one and the other." One of his severest critics with whom he carried on an extended correspondence said to him, "You do a great deal of harm, by breaking and setting aside order. For, order once ever so little set aside, confusion rushes in like a torrent." He answered, "What is the end of ecclesiastical order? Is it not to bring souls from the power of Satan to God; and to build them up in his fear and love? Order, then, is so far valuable, as it answers these ends; and if it answers them not, it is nothing worth. Now, I would fain know, where has order answered these ends? Not in any place where I have been; not among the tinners in Cornwall, the keelmen at Newcastle, the colliers in Kingswood or Staffordshire; not among the drunkards, swearers, Sabbath-breakers of Moorsfields, or the harlots of Drurylane. They could not be built up in the fear and love of God, while they were open, barefaced servants of the devil; and such they continued notwithstanding the most orderly preaching both in St. Luke's and St. Giles's Church. One reason whereof was, they never came near the church; nor had any desire or design so to do, till, by what you term breach of order, they were brought to fear God, to love him, and keep his commandments. It was not, therefore, so much the want of order, as of the knowledge and love of God, which kept those poor souls for so many years in open bondage to a hard master. And, indeed, wherever the knowledge and love of God are, true order will not be wanting. But the most Apostolical order, where these are not, is less than nothing and vanity." Here again, the fine balance of Wesley's mind is seen in his evaluation of the form and the power of religion. He was a stickler for form but a foe of formality. Form is a body; formality is a corpse. Methodism is Methodism as it fully senses this distinction. The mind loving God and therefore divinely illuminated, is in the Wesleyan tradition.

3. The love that warms the heart and illuminates the mind also empowers the will, and "thou shalt love the Lord thy God with all thy strength" is obeyed in the focusing of all the energies of the life upon this one thing, the

glorification of God in the work of rescuing the lost of earth. Wesley had no *natural* disposition to throw himself into an evangelistic crusade. In 1746, he said, "To this day, I have abundantly more temptation to lukewarmness than to impetuosity; to be a saunterer among Academic shades, a philosophical sluggard, than an itinerant preacher." Later he recalled that upon his return from America he "was in haste to retire to Oxford and bury himself in his beloved obscurity." It was the baptism of love upon all his powers that made him a ceaseless traveler in a world parish. He declared that in his Oxford days he lived almost the life of a hermit, and the declaration is confirmed by the correspond-ence he had with his father on the occasion of the father's effort to persuade him to be his successor at Epworth. With the mystical and cloistered ideal before his eyes he answered his father's proposal in a lengthy epistle, a few extracts from which will reveal the bent of his mind. He says, "When two ways of life are proposed, I would choose to consider first, which I have reason to believe will be best for *my own* soul," ... "And I believe the state wherein I am, will most forward me in this, because of the peculiar advantages I now enjoy. The first of these is daily converse with my friends. I know no other place under heaven, where I can have some always at hand of the same judgment, and engaged in the same studies. ... Another blessing which I enjoy here, in a greater degree than I could expect elsewhere, is retirement. I have not only as much, but as little company as I please. Trifling visitants I have none. No one takes it into his head to come within my doors, unless I desire him, or he has business with me; and even then, as soon as his business is done, he immediately goes away. Both these blessings are greatly endeared to me when I spend but one week out of this place. The far greatest part of the conversation I meet with abroad, even with the better sort of men, turns on points that are quite wide of my purpose; that no way forward the end of my life," that is, to save his own soul. Then he goes on, "Freedom from care is yet another invaluable blessing; and where could I enjoy this as I do now? I hear of such a thing as the cares of the world, but I feel them not. . . . Here I can be without carefulness. I can 'attend upon the Lord without distraction.'" Then he insists, "What others could do, I could not. I could not stand my ground one month, against intemperance in sleep, self-indulgence in food, irregularity in study; against a general lukewarmness in my affections, and remissness in my actions; against a softness directly opposite to the character of a good soldier of Jesus Christ. And then, when my spirit was thus dissolved, I should be an easy prey to every temptation; then might the cares of the world and the desire of other things, roll back with a full tide upon me; and it would be no wonder, if, while I preached to others, I myself should be a castaway." "The point is, whether I shall or not work out my salvation." This hot-house plant of Oxford, protecting himself from every chill breath of temptation, after the great transformation, became a cedar of Lebanon facing the winds that blew from every quarter. It may be a mere coincidence, but a significant one, that Wesley inserted the above letter, which was written in 1734, in the Journal for 1739 immediately preceding these entries, "April 2. At four in the afternoon, I submitted to be yet more vile, and proclaimed in the highways the glad tidings of salvation, speaking from a little eminence in a ground adjoining the city to about three thousand people." "April 4. At Baptist Mills. . . . I offered the grace of God to about fifteen hundred persons." "April 8. At seven in the morning I preached to about a thousand persons at Bristol." "About five thousand were in the afternoon at Rose-Green among whom I stood and cried, 'If any man thirst let him come unto me and drink." "April 10. At Bath I offered to about a thousand souls the free grace of God to 'heal their backslidings,' and in the morning to (I believe) more than two thousand. I preached to about the same number at Baptist-Mills in the afternoon." "I explained at seven, to five or six thousand persons, the story of the Pharisee and the Publican. About three thousand were present at Hannam Mount. Between five and six we went to Rose-Green; it rained hard at Bristol, but not a drop fell upon us, while I declared to about five thousand, 'Christ our wisdom, and righteousness, and sanctification, and redemption.' "

And from that point on, for almost fifty years, his *Journal* is a record of unremitting, self-forgetting toil for the salvation of men. It stands out in striking contrast to the religious diaries and journals of many of his predecessors and successors which are often filled with evidences of morbid self-dissection. Wesley hardly ever refers directly to his own experience. He did not keep his finger on his pulse. He kept his hands too busy for that. He did not look at his own eyes in a mirror to see whether or not they had a healthy color. He fixed his eyes on Jesus the great Object of faith and in self-oblivion enjoyed perfect moral health. He had a "heart at leisure from itself to soothe and sympathize" with the needs of others. And bad capital has been made of this, even by some of the followers of Wesley. He did not declare his own experience in writing because it was not necessary. All of his contemporaries knew he professed the experience he preached. David Brainerd's diary is full of sighs and self-scrutiny. Wesley said of him, "There is a pattern of self-devotion and deadness to the world! But how much of his sorrow and pain had been prevented, if he had understood the doctrine of Christian Perfection! How many tears did he shed because it was impossible to be freed from sin." That is one of the most hypocritical things ever written unless Wesley enjoyed and professed the Christian Perfection he wished Brainerd might have possessed. It was this that made Wesley dead to self. "Into paint will I grind thee, my bride," said the mad artist in a poem, and Wesley ground all of the interests of life into paint that he might picture Christ to the multitudes everywhere. He said, "If ever I should listen to that siren song, 'Spare thyself,' I believe my Master would spare me no longer, but soon take me away." He made a sizeable fortune in his life and poured it all into the work that was near his heart. At fifty-one years of age, believing he was dying, he wrote his own epitaph, "to prevent vile panegyric" after his death, as he explained, and these are the words, "Here lieth the body of John Wesley, a brand plucked out of the burning: who died of a consumption in the fifty-first year of his age, not leaving, after his debts are paid, ten pounds behind him: praying, God be merciful to me an unprofitable servant!" and then was raised up to preach the gospel thirty-seven years longer. Through all those years he consumed his substance on the altar of sacrificial service without talking about his sacrifice.

He redeemed the time by filling it with energetic labor for his Lord. He and leisure took leave of each other early in life, as he said, and the only reason he gave for not doing some things was that he did not have time for them. When his enemies assailed him, he said, "I have not time to answer every one who takes a fancy to nibble at John Wesley." In two successive Journal entries he tells of his failure to take some needed medicine because he had no time to do it since he was so busy about the work of the Kingdom. Dr. Samuel Johnson, one of the leading lights of literature in that day, complained to Patty Wesley, of her brother, "I hate to meet John Wesley. The dog enchants you with his conversation, and then breaks away to go and visit some old woman. This is very disagreeable to a man who loves to fold his legs and have his talk out as I do." But helping an old woman toward heaven was more important to John Wesley than talking with one of the most brilliant conversationalists of his time. One of his contemporaries, not a Methodist, wrote, "To one great purpose he dedicated his powers of body and mind; for this he relinquished all honor and preferment. At all times and in all places, in season and out of season, by gentleness, by terror, by argument, by persuasion, by reason, by interest, by every motive and every inducement, he strove, with unwearied assiduity, to turn men from the error of their ways and awaken them to virtue and religion. To the bed of sickness, or the couch of prosperity; to the prison or the hospital; to the house of mourning or the house of feasting, wherever there was a friend to serve or a soul to save, he readily repaired. He thought no office too humiliating, no condescension too low, no undertaking too arduous, to reclaim the meanest of God's offspring. The souls of all men were of equal value in his sight and the salvation of the immortal creature unutterably precious."

This was the method of Wesley and this was the method of Methodism. The love of Christ was the full head of steam that drove the wheels of spiritual commerce in early Wesleyanism. The word of God was like fire shut up in the bones of the primitive Methodists. It must have vent. They did not go because they were authorized or commanded to go. They marched to the heartbeats of love. They went out into the highways and hedges and compelled the people to come in through the compulsion of love. It was a modern Methodist who said, "The time has come when the church may have to leave her gorgeous temples and take to the road as early Methodism did." When the church walks the road leading toward the lost, the lost walk the road leading toward the church. It will take a wholly redeemed church to bring the redemptive message to the whole world.

Chapter 4

A HERITAGE FROM EARLY FREE METHODISM

Every spiritual movement has definite lines of connection
with the living past. The members of the so-called "silent
majority" are not so silent, for they being dead yet speak.
There are voices calling out of the centuries gone, projecting
the deposit of holy tradition and sound doctrine into our day.
There are saintly figures on the horizon back of us flashing
the light of their godly example upon our path. Something
of immense value has been transmitted to us. A rich legacy
of influence is ours. We are heirs of all the ages. A cry is
sounding from heaven, "Hearken to me ye that follow after
righteousness, ye that seek the Lord: look unto the rock
whence ye are hewn, and to the hole of the pit whence ye
are digged. Look unto Abraham your father and unto Sarah
that bare you: for I called him alone and blessed him and
increased him." A study of our ancestral backgrounds spiritually, will richly repay us. The young Elishas standing on the
path from which the old Elijahs have ascended, realizing
that these men were the standing army of God, "the chariots
of Israel and the horsemen thereof," should cry continually
"Let a double portion of their spirit be upon me." We are
in the true prophetic and apostolic succession if we have the
old prophetic and apostolic faith. Peter understood the far-
reaching purpose of Pentecost when he said to the multitude
present at the inauguration of the Spirit, "The promise is
unto you, and to your children, and to all that are afar off,
even as many as the Lord our God shall call." But the faith
once delivered unto the saints could not be taken across the

years over a smooth road. It had to be preserved and perpetu- ated at great cost. The path of its progress was intercepted repeatedly, and its bearers had to suffer, but with unshrinking fortitude the recipients of the great salvation blazed trails and cast up highways toward the future generations at the price of toil and tears, possessions and blood, reputation and life. Tradition honors all of the original apostles, save one, with martyr crowns, and even *he* could not live a long life without knowing the loneliness of banishment and the pain of punishment for his testimony. Stephen was propagating the faith when he became a victim of official murderers, but as he went down under the shower of stones his inner man towered heavenward and saw Jesus standing at the right hand of God to welcome him, and in the spirit of his Master he prayed for his murderers, "Lord lay not this sin to their charge." That prayer became a hook in the jaw of a young Pharisee by the name of Saul, who stood by, and as he went toward Damascus breathing out threatening and slaughter against the infant Church he came to the end of the line. He was smitten to the earth and bowed in submission at the revelation of Jesus Christ. The erstwhile raging perse- cutor became the earnest champion of the faith he had tried to exterminate. But he was to be shown what great things he must suffer for Christ's sake. He once declared that he knew not what should befall him in the future, only he had this testimony that everywhere bonds and affliction awaited him. But he carried the treasure on, through scourings and beat- ings, through stonings and shipwrecks, through long journey- ings, through perils of waters, perils of robbers, perils by his own countrymen, perils by the heathen, perils in the city, perils in the wilderness, perils in the sea, perils among false brethren, through weariness and painfulness, through watchings and fastings, through hunger and thirst, through cold and nakedness. What a biography! And yet he transferred the deposit unimpaired to Timothy, his son in the faith, saying joyfully, "I have fought a good fight, I have finished my course, I have kept the faith." The first three centuries of the Christian era were one prolonged period of persecution, but there were those faithful unto death, who kept up the contact so the message could come through. When the dark ages mantled the world the Waldenses kept the light aglow on their Alpine heights through thirty-three successive wars by which their enemies sought to destroy them. Then the German monk, Martin Luther, laboriously plowing in the field of the church in quest of peace struck his plowshare against the corner of the casket in which the treasure of truth was hid, and this spark flashed out, "The just shall live by faith." He was awakened. Upon the advice of others he went to Rome to climb Pilate's staircase on his knees in the continued search for peace. Again his plow struck the casket, and again the spark of light flashed out, "The just shall live by faith." He continued to plow, and on the next round the share got under the casket and turned it up to pour its treasures at his feet. Then he went out to nail his ninety-five theses on the door of the cathedral in Wittenberg and preach justification by faith. He defied devils, and authorities civil and ecclesiastical. When threatened and ordered to recant, he stood like Gibraltar with the mad waves breaking at its base, and replied without fear, "Here I stand. I can do no other. God help me." The world is indebted to Luther for that stand. Bishop John F. Hurst said that "in an old Hussite hymn book in the university library of Prague there are three most suggestive illuminations. In one John Wyclif is striking sparks from a stone; in the second John Hus is kindling coals with the sparks; in the third Martin Luther is brandishing a flaming torch. Thus does the old scribe picture the true relation of the English, Bohemian, and German Reformations." But the fire of the successive Reformations had burned low at the time John Wesley arose. George Cookman, the father of the Sainted Alfred Cookman, once described in a vivid word picture the religious situation in England in the middle of the 18th century. He compares the religious life of England at that time to a great, cold cathedral in the center of which, on the stone floor, a fire is smouldering, and a few shivering worshippers are gathered closely round endeavoring to keep warm. Suddenly a man short of stature walks briskly up to the fire and begins to stir it vigorously and clear away the ashes. That man is John Wesley. Another man appears with a countenance like that of an angel, carrying bundles of faggots under his arms. He places the faggots on the coals. That man is John Fletcher, the great defender of the Wesleyan teaching. Another man appears on the scene, portly of build, and serious in appearance. He stoops and blows at the coals until the faggots kindle. That man is George Whitefield, with his heaven-inspired eloquence. Another man appears with a harp in his hand and as the flame ascends and spreads, he sings,

> 1. See how great a flame aspires
>   Kindled by a spark of grace
>   Jesus love the nations fires
>   Sets the kingdoms in a blaze.

2. To bring fire, on earth He came,
   Kindled in some heart it is
   O that all might taste and see
   All partake the glorious bliss.

That man is Charley Wesley the sweet singer of Methodism. These men and a thousand helpers lighted their torches at this flame and went forth to kindle countless revival fires across England, Ireland, Scotland and Wales. But they were branded by the clergy and hounded by the mob. They were held up to scorn in the press. As late as 1809, when Methodism was well established in England, the frivolous ecclesiastic, Sydney Smith, heaped scorn on those who objected to the unjust opposition he had excited against the Methodists. He replied to their objections by saying, "It is not the practice with destroyers of vermin to allow the little victims a veto upon the weapons used against them. If this were otherwise, we should have one set of vermin banishing small-tooth combs; and another protesting against mouse-traps; a third prohibiting the finger and thumb; a fourth exclaiming against the intolerable infamy of using soap and water. It is impossible, however, to listen to such pleas. They must all be caught, killed, and cracked, in the manner and by the instruments which are found most efficacious to their destruction; and the more they cry out, the greater plainly is the skill used against them." But Methodism marched on amid reproach and shame, and carried the cross triumphantly.

The fire it had kindled leaped across the Atlantic, and exactly 100 years before the organization of the Free Methodist Church, Philip Embury landed in New York and conducted the first Methodist service in America, with a congregation of five present, and shortly after built the first Methodist Church in America. From that insignificant mustard seed sprang a great tree, which took deep root and spread its branches over the land. Then strange birds began to build their nests in its boughs. The church had prospered spiritually and numerically, but in her prosperity she courted favor with the world. In the merger which followed, the worldly side of the partnership assumed the dictatorial role, and the protesting minority of Spirit-filled men was subjected to systematic persecution and excommunication.

I. CONTENTION FOR THE PRINCIPLES OF HOLINESS WAS THE OCCASION FOR THE EXPULSION OF THE FOUNDERS OF FREE METHODISM FROM THE MOTHER CHURCH. In this, history simply repeated itself. Contrary principles inevitably come into conflict, especially when they are forced into close proximity with each other. Never do they come to such close quarters as in the religious world and there they clash fiercely. The first war, in heaven, and the first murder on earth grew out of the issue between sin and holiness. The history of the church is the repeated story of the Spirit's presidency as sole Vicar of God in his chosen earth-temple, until carnal men with carnal schemes and dreams have driven him out and He has re-incarnated himself in some obscure, repudiated body of consecrated people. When a worldly majority in any church rejects the life and power of godliness an irrepressible conflict is precipitated, and out of the travail comes a re-birth of holy principles to be propagated in the power of the Holy Ghost, through a new medium.

Long before the worldly contingent in the Genesee Conference of the Methodist Episcopal Church had become strong enough to strike effective blows against the work of holiness, prominent men had observed with deep grief of heart the drift away from the original standards of Wesleyanism. American Methodism never produced a purer or mightier spirit than Bishop L. L. Hamline. He had said on one occasion when someone complained that a certain preacher made holiness his hobby, "Woe to the Methodist preacher, that son of perdition, who *does not* make holiness his hobby." For years before the series of events in the Genesee Conference which led to the organization of the Free Methodist Church, Bishop Hamline recorded in his journals the anguish of a soul torn by the declensions from primitive doctrine and piety. He states after one of his Episcopal visitations to the Genesee Conference, "The young preachers of the conference have been captured by Zinzendorfism." Zinzendorf denied that there was any need of a second work of grace to purify the heart. Some of the young preachers referred to by Hamline were no doubt associated with the group which a few years later launched the wholesale attack against all of the preachers who contended for the doctrine of entire sanctification as a second work of grace.

God had his providential man ready to raise an alarm. B. T. Roberts a man of strong intellect and clear spiritual vision wrote a series of articles on "New School Methodism," for the *Northern Independent,* a paper edited by Rev. Wm. Hosmer, a man who was interested in the perpetuation of original Methodism. In these articles Mr. Roberts set side by side two photographs. One was the photograph of unadulterated Methodism and the other was a photograph

77

of Methodism compromising and modifying her standard to please the worldly-minded. He showed clearly that the two photographs would not stereoscope into one harmonious picture. The antagonism was irreconcilable. The enemies of holiness were enraged. Charges were preferred against B. T. Roberts. He was tried for "unchristian and immoral conduct" because he contended for the high principles of Christianity and opposed the very things which lead to immoral conduct. He was found guilty of the charges preferred against him, and in the face of the verdict was sent to an appointment. During the following year a man by the name of George Estes re-published the articles on "New School Methodism" with an account of Roberts' trial appended. Roberts was charged with contumacy for having re-published the articles and although Estes testified that he alone was responsible for the publication and circulation of the articles, Roberts was found guilty and expelled from the church. He appealed to the ensuing session of the General Conference. The appeal was denied by that body. When the appeal was turned down Roberts said, "I appeal to God and the people." Laymen who had been members of the Methodist Church for many years were read out of the church by the score simply because they protested against the highhanded political tactics that were being used to crush the heralds of Bible holiness.

The animus of all these proceedings is not difficult to determine. Although charged with "immoral and unchristian conduct" not even his most bitter opponents ever believed Roberts to be guilty. After being pronounced guilty at his first trial, Roberts was sent to an appointment. Although being found guilty of contumacy at his second

78

trial without a shred of evidence to prove anything except his absolute innocence, the progress of the trial was suspended a full day while a memorial service was conducted in honor of Rev. Wm. Kendall who was also a subject of Conference manipulations and persecutions and was marked for expulsion at that very session, and Roberts was unanimously selected as the one to preach the sermon on that occasion. During the trial some of the preachers were absent. Without hearing the testimony in the case they voted to sustain the charges, having agreed in secret session to sustain them before the case was tried. Several of those who voted with the majority later said in substance, "Well, if the charges were not sustained by sufficient proof, the Conference served them right, for they are great agitators and promoters of disorder and fanaticism." That reveals they were trying Roberts and others of like mould on one charge and convicting them on another. Their hatred was against the preaching of holiness and the spiritual results of such preaching. Thomas Carleton, one of the most intense enemies of the persecuted preachers said, "I would rather meet a thousand devils any time than three Nazarites," as the holiness group was branded. Whether Carleton referred to a particular three or not, it is a fact that three men were particularly hated and feared by the anti-holiness group in the church; namely, Roberts with his unanswerable logic; Loren Stiles with his mighty eloquence; and Joseph McCreery with his keen Irish wit, all baptized with the Holy Ghost. McCreery touched the heart of the matter when he said in his quaint Irish way, "Some of the younger boys have taken my mother, the Methodist Church, in her old age, painted her face and curled her hair, hooped her, and flounced her and jeweled her, and fixed her up, until we could hardly tell her from a woman of the world. Now when I have taken the old lady, and washed her face, and straightened out her hair, and dressed her up in modest apparel, so that she looks like herself again, they make a great hue and cry, and call it abusing mother." The devoted and godly laymen of the Genesee Conference met in their second convention to consider ways and means to stop the wholesale excommunication of both preachers and members who stood for the old paths. In this convention held at Albion, N. Y., in 1859, they formulated a statement of their position and among other things said, "These repeated acts of expulsion, wrong as they are in themselves, deserve the stronger condemnation from the fact, scarcely attempted to be disguised, that the object is to prevent the work of holiness from spreading among us—to put down the life and power of godliness in our churches, and to inaugurate in its stead the peaceable reign of a cold and heartless formalism—in short, to do away with what has always been a distinctive feature of Methodism. If the work which the men who were expelled both this year and last have labored, and not without success, to promote be 'fanaticism' then has Methodism from the beginning been 'fanaticism.' "

These trials were like the farcical mistrials of Jesus. He was charged with blasphemy and treason and was executed as a criminal, but the real reason for his crucifixion was that his holy teaching and holy character were a rebuke to worldliness and formality in the church. The Jews cried for the blood of the Son of God and at the same time demanded that Barrabas, a notorious robber, be released. The very conference which voted Roberts and others out of the pale

80

of the church, voted to re-admit a man who had previously been expelled for wrong conduct, and this man was guilty of gross imprudence, or worse, during the sitting of this conference. The very General Conference which refused to hear Roberts' appeal heard the appeal of a man who had been guilty of positive immorality on more than one occasion and sustained the appeal, restoring him to good standing.

So on the issue of holiness the persecuted were excommunicated ecclesiastically, but the Genesee Conference excommunicated itself spiritually from the fellowship of God's elect ones and lost 1,000 members during the next ten years.

In justice it should be said that in 1910, more than fifty years after the events we have delineated, the Genesee Conference of the Methodist Church, at its annual session, voted to restore the credentials of B. T. Roberts to his son Professor B. H. Roberts. If the patterns of original Methodism could have been restored to the Genesee Conference at the same time, it would have been a cause of rejoicing both on the part of the mother and her daughter.

II. POSSESSION OF THE SPIRIT OF HOLINESS WAS THE BASIS OF COMMUNION BETWEEN THE MEMBERS OF THE PERSECUTED COMPANY. The very spirit which was repulsive to their enemies became the bond of unity between those who have obtained "like precious faith." It was not a matter of political partisanship, but of spiritual fellowship. They did not represent a formal constituency, but a holy communion. They loved one another with a pure heart fervently. They flowed together and their hearts were enlarged. They were accused of having a secret society under the name of "Nazarites." There was an element of unsuspected truth in the charge. These so-called "Nazarites" were members in good standing in the ancient and honorable order of the sons of God, and the secret of the Lord was with them. They were divinely initiated into the mysteries of the kingdom of heaven, the deep things of God, by the mighty baptism of the Holy Ghost. They knew the pass words. They understood each other's language. There are deep moral affinities between the saints. There is a law of spiritual gravitation, even in this world by which every man goes to his own place and company. Every child in the family of God recognizes the family resemblance in others who have been born of the Spirit, and is strangely drawn to them. When Thomas LaDue, a man mighty in word and in deed, identified himself with the Free Methodist Church he said that he came into her communion "as naturally as a bird flies to its nest." He was guided by the homing instinct of the wholly sanctified. He was at home in the congenial atmosphere of holy lives. Pentecostal companies have always been of one heart and one soul. The living stones cemented together with love seem to be *more* closely united under the pressure of persecution. Elias Bowen, a prominent preacher of the Oneida Conference, who had been a Presiding Elder in that Conference for 24 years, had been a ministerial delegate to the General Conference seven times, and had been urged by his friends to permit his name to be used as a candidate for the bishopric, although, having never met the men who were being so unjustly used in the Genesee Conference, was able to see from the nature of the written assaults upon them that they were being opposed because they stood for Wesleyan holiness. He came to their defense by publishing articles in which he approved of their work, and unsparingly condemned the actions that had been taken against them. When the Susquehanna Conference of the Free Methodist Church was formed, it was not long until Bowen joined that conference, a man full of days and enjoying the highest honors, save one, that the Methodist Episcopal Church could have bestowed upon him, yet choosing to close his pilgrim days in the fellowship of the new church which had nothing great to offer him. He said when he asked the Susquehanna Conference to receive him, "I have been a Free Methodist for more than fifty years." The father of S. K. J. Chesbrough was a member of the Methodist Church at Pekin, N. Y. Roberts was sent as pastor to the church where Chesbrough belonged, from the conference which found him guilty of "unchristian and immoral conduct." A prominent preacher in the conference had informed the people against Roberts before his arrival and he met with a very cool reception. Father Chesbrough had decided he would not go to hear him preach. He said, "What have we done that a man convicted of immoral conduct should be sent as our preacher?" When Sabbath morning came, however, he reversed his decision since he was in the habit of attending worship regularly. He said, "It can do no hurt to hear him once anyway." As he was returning from the service with his son, he rode for over a mile in silence and then said, "Well, Sam, I know nothing about the man, but I do know that what we have heard today is Methodism as I used to hear it in the old Baltimore Conference, and as I have not heard it preached in Western New York." That first contact with Roberts told Chesbrough that here was one whose heart was in tune with the divinest music of his own soul. They were drawn into most intimate and precious fellowship and the son took a prominent part in the beginning of Free Methodism. One layman who found his way into the Free Methodist fold said, "I knew my mother's voice when I heard it."

In such a communion a church trial would be a rare necessity. The reason is that an intensely spiritual movement is always self-disciplining and self-purifying in a high degree. We have insisted that there are deep affinities for all that is holy and heavenly in a pure heart. There are antipathies, just as deep, against the holy and heavenly in a carnal heart. The white heat of spirituality maintained in a church will draw the pure gold to its center; all else will be driven from the vicinity of the holy flame. In such circumstances there is not much need for official chimney sweeps to clean the chimney out by vigorous disciplinary applications. The soot gathers in the chimney in the first place because of imperfect combustion in the furnace. A smoky, smouldering fire is responsible for the choked condition of the chimney. A flaming fire will keep a clean chimney clean, and a flaming fire started where a feeble one has been burning will burn a dirty chimney out. The church at Ephesus had to resort to church trials to get rid of heretics when she left her first love. "The church that is holy is armed with a perpetual decree of excision against the hypocritical and profane and unclean," said Dr. A. J. Gordon.

III. THE CONSUMING PASSION OF HOLINESS WAS THE STIMULUS OF THE AGGRESSON OF OUR FATHERS ON THE WORLD. There were no rewards to attract and stimulate the founders of the Free Methodist Church. They had given up all prospects of churchly preferment in the prime of life, when excluded from the bosom of the church they loved. There were no large churches awaiting them, with the promise of big salaries to remunerate them for their toils. They took the responsibility of evangelizing large areas without a church in which to preach or a house in which to live. They had no strong base of operations. They had to originate a base from which to work. They had to *create* societies and *build* churches and parsonages. They had to *win* a membership, not by proselyting but by effective evangelism. The question could never be "What will I get out of this?" The burning question was always, "What can I put into this." At the call of God they went singing,

> Lord obediently we'll go
> Gladly leaving all below,
> Only thou our leader be,
> And we still will follow thee.

They took the world for their parish. They seized every opportunity to spread Scriptural holiness. They sometimes *made* opportunities where there seemed to be none. They were instant in season, out of season. They invested their lives in a seemingly feeble cause, and went on at the risk of their all. They were not driven by the coercive power of an outward lash but by the compulsions of an inward life. Our sainted Bishop E. P. Hart was speaking out of ample observation and experience when he said some years ago that "God, when calling laborers into his vineyard does not speak down into a dead-house with its shelves of spiritual mummies embalmed in the odor of a dead sanctity, calling upon them to do their duty or double their diligence, but he first calls them to life." More abundant life made our fathers abundant in labors. They did not win their way by flattery, for their message pierced like a javelin and searched like an X-ray. They were kind in spirit and gentlemanly in bearing, but they were not men-pleasers on the highest issues of existence. They did not smooth down the rough text to ears polite, nor apologize for any of the Spirit's work. They opposed popular and pleasant sins wherever they met them. The writer has heard John La Due, of precious memory, tell, in a reminiscent mood, of hearing Bishop Hart many years ago assailing one of the popular sins of the time and discerning how the truth was going home he said, "Well this sermon may not have many heads but I hope it has some points." Sometimes people become angry at such preaching, but went away with arrows of conviction in the soul that drank up the spirits until they returned to pray and repent. It was not the popularity of the message that made it stick, but the holy passion of the messenger born in a heart perfectly loyal to God.

IV. THE SUPREME BLISS OF HOLINESS WAS THE SOURCE OF THE INSPIRATION OF OUR FOUNDING FATHERS. The highway of holiness is the main street of heaven extended into earthly territory. Along that highway the celestial commerce travels. Over that road the heavenly products are imported. Sometimes they come in such measure as to be unspeakable and full of glory, blessings so big there is not room enough to receive them. The load of the divine may be so great that our finite scales cannot weigh it and our best description of it is that it represents an "exceeding weight of glory." "Blessed are the pure in heart." Holiness is out of the heart of "the blessed God" and conveys some of His bliss to human hearts. Heaven is holiness above. Holiness is heaven below. "Celestial fruit on earthly ground from faith and hope may grow," and the pilgrim travelers may march toward Zion with songs and everlasting joy on their heads. Our fathers knew this profound joy and as a consequence they knew the difference between something pumped up and something poured down. They knew the difference between the waves of surface feeling which are set in motion by the passing breezes of animal excitement, resulting in the hilarious hurrahs of religious sentimentalism, and the great tides that are perpetually lifted by something in the heavens taking hold of the heart of man with its deep moving currents. Sometimes there is a solemn joy "too full for sound or foam," and a man is held in the spell of "a speechless awe that dare not move, and all the silent heaven of love." Our fathers felt *that*, and so when they were sorrowful they were yet rejoicing. The fountain could not be sealed up by tribulation or persecution. Through shadow and sunshine the hidden stream flowed on. Reproduce this scene in your mind. It is the year 1856. The Genesee Conference of the Methodist Episcopal Church is in session. The process of crushing the holiness preachers has started but many of the people are not aware of it until the appointments are read. William Kendall has been appointed by the conference to a weak circuit where it is hoped he will be starved into submission, and others have been similarly treated. After the appointments are read the presiding Bishop, detecting the sad spirit of the congregation, asks if someone will start a song. William Kendall, rising above the depressing atmosphere through a fresh look at the eternal, with his beautiful tenor voice starts singing,

87

> "Come on my partners in distress,
> My comrades through this wilderness,
> Who still your bodies feel.
> Awhile forget your griefs and fears
> And look beyond this vale of tears
> To that celestial hill."

The Bishop says, "Let us pray," but Kendall, not hearing the call to prayer, continues the song,

> "Beyond the bounds of time and space
> Look forward to that heavenly place,
> The saints secure abode.
> On faith's strong eagle pinions rise
> And force your passage to the skies
> And scale the mount of God."

Again the Bishop says, "Let us pray," but Kendall is lost in his singing and the congregation is beginning to catch his victorious spirit. They continue:

> "Who suffer with our Master here
> We shall before his face appear
> And by his side sit down.
> To patient faith the prize is sure,
> And all that to the end endure
> The cross, shall wear the crown.
>
> Thrice blessed, bliss-inspiring hope!
> It lifts the fainting spirits up,
> It brings to life the dead.
> Our conflicts here will soon be past,

And you and I ascend at last,
Triumphant with our Head.

That great mysterious Deity
We soon with open face shall see:
The beatific sight
Shall fill the heavenly courts with praise,
And wide diffuse the golden blaze
Of everlasting light."

With hearts aglow and heads lifted the persecuted band went out and wrought for God, the Spirit working with them, and gracious revivals crowned their efforts. When Kendall came to die he said, "I have been swimming in the waters of death for four days already, and they are like sweet incense all around me." So these saintly nightingales sang their songs in the darkness and storm. Such men built enduring foundations for the future.

We have entered into their labors. We are legatees of the glorious past in which they made history for God. But we are also trustees for the present generation and for the future. Shall we hand the heritage on as pure as we received it, or shall we be the unworthy sons and daughters of worthy fathers, and let the inheritance run to waste, or sell it out to the highest bidder? Shall we face a skeptical age with a stammering, hesitant testimony as we come along in the wake of men who faced their generation with clear trumpet-tongued testimony? Shall we walk with delicate, halting steps, fearing lest we tread on some pet sin of a people in highhanded rebellion against God, in a world where our fathers went straight and marched with the tread of giants shaking the kingdom of evil? Shall we feed on the mere crumbs that fall from the table where others sat in the past and fed on the strong meat, and drank the wine of the kingdom until they were strong enough to wrestle victoriously with the most colossal problems? Shall we cover ourselves with the ashes of a cold altar, and mourn sentimentally over the indifference of the world, when our spiritual progenitors kept the fire burning so hotly that men were too uncomfortable to be indifferent? Shall the stream of our spiritual life trickle thinly among the pebbles of triviality, too weak to survive the beginning of a drought, after a generation of men whose spiritual life was like a mighty river dashing and roaring through the mountains, and among the boulders of great issues, and flowed with vast volume through the arid regions, turning the deserts into gardens despite the burning wastes of unspirituality around them? If we do, we shall have mocked our privileges and dishonored God. We shall be feeble and our spiritual progeny will be more feeble. The church will then have only a past. When a church has nothing but a past spiritually, she has no spiritual future. Her children will be born dead. Let us keep faith with our fathers! Let us keep the fire glowing with our whole burnt offerings. Let us hold the banner aloft, unfurled to every breeze. Let us keep the armor on and refuse to be mere camp-followers. Let us live under the anointing which teacheth. Let us be men and women of prayer. Let us properly serve our generation. If we do, we shall make a lasting impression upon the world and Christ shall see of the travail of his soul and be satisfied. In 1955 the writer received a personal letter from an Episcopalian rector. Among other things he wrote,

"I do not write this to flatter you or your people, but simply to express the devout hope that the candle of the Lord which burns in your midst may never be permitted to become dim. . . . The pure doctrines of original Methodism and the primitive simplicity of the piety which your Zion has preserved, have made your people what they are. . . . Neither doctrines nor forms nor polities can save a church from stagnation and death. I . . . hope that, in the zeal for adaptation to the necessities of the times in meeting the appalling need which confronts the church, the old economy may not be sacrificed. The passion for modernity is all about us, and the purest of people is not immune to it. I firmly believe that when your founding fathers went out under the stars and laid the foundations for a church which would preserve the essentials of Methodism they builded better than they knew. . . . May the Lord grant . . . that your connection may be preserved in all its integrity to stand forth clothed with righteousness, anointed with the Spirit of Holiness and of Power, imbued with the spirit of your fathers, a connection whose sleepless aim is to win souls to Christ and spread scriptural holiness through these United States."

The writer shares this high hope expressed by an outside observer. But its fruition will cost us something, as it cost our fathers something.

The renowned pianist, Paderewski has told in his autobiography of how he played in twenty-two consecutive concerts with an infected wound on one of his fingers that made every performance a perfect agony and when he had finished each concert the keys of the piano were red with blood. He played thus against his doctor's orders, who had told him he was taking his life in his hands. The unconquerable spirit of the pianist which was determined to fulfill the expectations of the people and get the music out carried him through. If we get the music of the gospel to our generation it will cost us some agony of spirit and the keys will be red with sacrificial blood. But it will be our joy and crown of rejoicing to know we have reached those who needed the message. The Holy Spirit can give us the indomitable will to carry on and carry through.

Chapter 5

THE HERITAGE PRESERVED

An exhortation from Paul to Timothy, his "son in the faith," will serve as a suitable consideration in which to saturate the whole message. It is found in II Timothy 1:4, and I am quoting from Weymouth's translation. "That precious truth which is entrusted to you, guard through the Holy Spirit who has his home in your hearts."

It would be most fitting for us to begin with the humble admission that everything we possess in the Christian faith is a divine revelation and gift. In the realm of spiritual reality we may properly ask, "What have we that we have not received?" We are not originators or creators; we are recipients of a donation originating in the unmerited love of God. "Every good gift and every perfect gift is from above and cometh down from the Father of lights with whom is no variableness neither shadow of turning." Our faith is the "wisdom from above," once and for all "*delivered* unto the saints," and not *discovered* or *developed* by sinners. Man is morally and spiritually bankrupt by nature, and only by grace can he be put in possession of the treasure that will make him rich forever, if he wills.

Everything hinges on that phrase, "if he wills." While we have no power to create a saving religion, we have the responsibility of cooperating with the great divine Giver in such a manner as to receive and preserve that which has been committed to us. We are always in danger of losing the faith while we slumber at ease in Zion. We may sell it to the highest bidder, or even to the lowest bidder if he is loudest in his bidding. We may give it away as something antiquated and irrelevant, in the name of progress. The text warns against these dangers. We have something entrusted to us that is worth guarding with sleepless vigilance at the cost of our lives.

I. There is precious truth in an old creed to be preserved in belief.

Those who embrace the widespread creed of creedlessness, like Julian Huxley's "Religion Without Revelation," beginning with the affirmation, "I believe in God, the *creature* Almighty," show an unconcealed distaste for Christian doctrine. They identify it with dry abstractions and speculative air castles. They would turn the whole vast realm of religious belief into a vacuum, emptied of the supposedly illusive theoretical vision, by the magic dictum of modern materialism, "Exclusively abstract structures must vanish." Whatever may be said of the homemade theologies that have come and gone like a procession of specters, sound Bible doctrine is not an exclusively abstract structure. It has roots reaching down to streams springing from eternal sources and shoots pushing up through the solid strata of all history. Our creedal statements, however sketchy, are pictures of historical fact.

The science of astronomy did not create the heavens; the heavens created the science of astronomy. The astronomer takes observations, photographs the skies, then constructs a celestial chart and records his findings in astronomical teaching. So sound doctrine is the portrait or map of objective reality in the moral and spiritual firmament, and not the projection of bright notions from ingenious brains into an

94

imaginary sky like the stars projected against an artificial dome by the complicated machine in the Adler Planetarium at Chicago. The Apostles did not follow cunningly devised fables of their own or another's making. Their teachings were not the recorded echoes of their own soliloquies while in a religious frenzy. Our faith fixes upon facts, and not upon so-called fancies of prophetic or apostolic subjectivity.

More dangerous than the creed of the no-creedist is the corruption and perversion of sound doctrine, turning the truth of God into a lie. Some would wave aside the whole matter of doctrinal differences as lightly as did the Irish wit who said, "Protestants take their religion *a la carte* while Catholics take theirs *table d'hote*." But the difference is much deeper than that. It is a difference in the bill of fare. The Catholic menu has large measures of pagan poison mixed with some of the great fundamentals of the faith, plus invented dogmas that are as corrupt as the day-old manna of the Israelites. Every heresy, Catholic or Protestant, however attractive, is a fragile fig leaf apron manufactured to cover the shame of sin.

Get the central sun of truth right and you will have the subordinate planets right. Central and all-pervasive in history is the outworking of the plan of salvation. Central in that plan is the person of Jesus Christ as Savior and Lord. The transfiguration scene is a condensed revelation of God's eternal purpose, an epitome of redemptive history. To this sublime meeting place of heaven and earth Moses and Elias came up as if from past history to acknowledge the Lord of the Law and the Prophets. The law functioned as a schoolmaster to lead men to Christ. It brought the knowledge of sin and awakened a sense of the need of a deliverer. The ceremonial law shadowed forth the sacrificial atonement to be effected on Calvary once and for all. The sole mission of the Jewish people was to be the national forerunner of Christ in all their typical services until the personal forerunner should come crying, "Behold the lamb of God." The prophets saw the fulfillment of the promise "afar off," and with the long arms of faith eliminated the space of centuries and "embraced" the reality. To the transfiguration, Peter, James and John came up as if from the future of the Holy Ghost dispensation to acknowledge the "Author of eternal salvation." "Jesus only" filled their eyes at the close. The cross, by anticipation, stood in the midst of the glory, for the decease to be accomplished at Jerusalem was the dominant theme of conversation on the "holy mount."

The crucified Christ is the focus of all redemptive facts and the fountain of all redeeming forces. Paul would know nothing but Jesus Christ and Him crucified. He would glory in nothing but the cross. He would preach nothing but Christ crucified as the consummate demonstration of the wisdom and power of God. This exclusive choice of Paul was not narrowness, for the atoning Christ is *the* Truth," "*the* Light of the world." All light radiates from the cross. All attraction is toward the cross. The Christ suspended on the cross gives us a proper conception of man's nature and possibilities. His assumption of our nature being permanent, and not simply a temporary expedient for the purpose of making death a possible experience to Him, gives us a doctrine of man that elevates him immeasurably above the brutes. The beastly philosophy that tends to degrade man was keenly characterized by a noted scholar as teaching that "By necessary laws primitive matter has developed into a great synthesis of things rising into a tall pyramid of which, by conditions favorable to him, man, the *ex-ape*, is the *apex*." Is man a little higher than other animals or "a little lower than the angels"? "The man, Christ Jesus," who almost invariably called himself "the Son of man," is the answer. The incarnation was supernatural in its mode, but the union between the human and the divine was not unnatural. The Son of God could come in the likeness of man, for man was originally made in the likeness of God. Despite man's depravity, God recognizes in him, as Dr. Whedon said many years ago, "A sublime excellence, both of substance and structure." The temple is polluted and full of idols, but it still has the capacity to house God. The incarnation proves it. The gold still has intrinsic value, although the divine image on it has been defaced and the divine superscription obliterated. The price paid for its recovery proves it. Man is worth saving. "The precious blood" was not shed to save a "fearfully and wonderfully made" piece of physical mechanism, "the aristocrat of animals," with an ultimate destiny of dust in prospect. It was shed to redeem the invaluable and imperishable gem of moral and spiritual personality. However terribly lost, "the diamond cannot rot," to use Victor Hugo's phrase.

The doctrine of sin receives its clearest exposition at the cross. Man's spiritual dignity is matched by his moral depravity. Man fell by sin and the fall was far. The depth of his descent is plumbed only by the passion and death of Christ. The writer to the Hebrews repeated the question of the Psalmist, "What is man that thou art mindful of him, or the son of man that thou visitest him?" when he observed this creature, once crowned with honor and glory and exercising

97

dominion over the works of God's hands, now dethroned and enslaved. "Now we see not yet all things put under him." "Things are in the saddle and ride mankind," as Emerson said. But the star of hope flashes athwart the night of sin to the bottom of the "horrible pit." "We see Jesus—glorious in his apparel and traveling in the greatness of his strength— mighty to save." But His garments are crimson with blood. He has trodden the wine press alone. He has tasted death for every man. The cost of the remedy reveals the strength of the malady. If the agony of Gethsemane means that Christ tasted our cup, and if the anguish of Calvary means that He touched our doom, sin is much more than a cutaneous infection to be cured by the application of various man-made salves and plasters. The serpent has bitten us and the poison works through our nature to paralyze the will, pervert the affections, and drive the reason to moral madness.

From the cross the complementary perfections of the Godhead pre-eminently shine. "Here the whole Deity is known." Man has ever been prone to mutilate the perfect picture of God and fancy a half-God who is *no* God. Heathenism with its fear-ridden conscience, conceives a cruel, implacable monster, ever ready to crush those who wilfully or inadvertently offend him. On the other hand, our brilliant contemporary paganism, called "civilization," intoxicated by pleasure, conceives a soft, smiling "domestic deity," an indulgent heavenly father, doting upon his weak, rather than wayward, children and more than willing to pardon the vices and crimes they have labeled "little human errors," without the ado of atonement or reparation. The heathen conception hopelessly dooms man while the modern, civilized conception dethrones God. On Golgotha the hand of justice strikes at sin and the hand of love grasps the sinner, while one heart of eternal holiness pulsates in both. Here "mercy and truth meet together, righteousness and peace kiss each other." Here "vengeance and compassion join in their divinest forms." Divine compassion does not mean divine connivance at sin, for God "spared not his own Son" when He voluntarily entered the region of the curse and identified himself with sinful man. He "*must* suffer" according to His own prediction. It is not possible for the cup to be removed from His lips. He cannot escape the blow of justice if He stands where it is to fall. "It pleased the Lord to bruise him: he hath put him to grief," and "made his soul an offering for sin." Divine justice is not divine cruelty for God "commends his love to us" at Calvary. There justice wrought with love to accomplish the ends of holiness.

The supreme deity of Christ came to fullest manifestation on the cross. When Christ seemed most helplessly human He proved Himself wholly divine. John beheld Him in the grand consummation with "many crowns" on the "sacred head once wounded." He won all of those crowns in His redeeming capacity on the cruel tree. He turned the cross into a throne and became the "King of all kingdoms." While the hands and feet of the human Jesus were nailed to the cross, as Lord of all created worlds the divine Christ lifted an infinite hand to cover the face of the sun, and trod the earth with the foot of supernatural power until it quaked. As King of "the unseen holy" He reached forth and rent the veil of the temple from top to bottom, opening the kingdom of heaven to all believers. As King of human hearts He melted the dying thief into penitence and swept away his guilty fears. As King of the realms of bliss He promised this same thief, "Today shalt thou be with me in Paradise," as if to say, "That world of blessedness belongs to me. I have the keys at my girdle. I open and no man shuts." As King of the City of Death He swung its gates back and awakened many of the saints out of their long sleep to appear in Jerusalem after His own resurrection. No wonder the iron-hearted centurion of Rome's iron legions exclaimed, "Truly this man was the Son of God."

When Jesus cried, "It is finished," the foundation was laid for the superstructural work of the Holy Ghost. After His resurrection, Christ showed the disciples His hands and side, and then breathing on them, said, "Receive ye the Holy Ghost." This was the first breath of the Pentecostal day that was soon to break in full power with "the sound as of a rushing, mighty wind." The gift of the Holy Ghost depended on the sacrificial death-wounds of Christ. Some time ago as we motored southward, the light of the westering sun made a blazing cross on the cloud that thinly veiled its face and the shining symbol seemed to be a part of the sun. Christ, the "Sun of righteousness," is the center of the gospel system of truth and the cross is the center of that Sun. So our creed is the creed of the cross.

II. There is precious truth in a new creation to be preserved in experience.

One of the most penetrating theologians of the last hundred years, P. T. Forsyth, said, "Even when we put the accent on the Cross, we may pronounce it wrong. We may shorten the saving Word. We may see but a partial cross." Many can talk glibly about the cross and what was done on the cross in our behalf two milleniums ago, without any knowledge of the "radiance streaming" from it and the "hallowed,

100

cleansing stream" flowing from it, working a revolutionary change in men here and now.

The historical manifestation of Christ was necessary to furnish the foundation for our faith, but if the mental contemplation of the "excellent glory" of that manifestation is the whole of our religion, it is a beautiful dream of the past and not a saving vision of the present, and doubt cannot be kept at bay. The flashing fireflies of liberalism accentuate, rather than relieve, the darkness of uncertainty. A spiritually defunct conservatism, holding the lamp of "sound words" in its hand, as a precious heirloom from the fathers, cannot make us sure when the light has gone out because the heart-vessel lacks the oil of the Spirit. The world is confirmed in its unbelief when it beholds professed believers holding a lightless lamp in a trembling hand while repeating the orthodox creed with a stammering voice.

When the belief of the mind issues in the trust of the heart, "the day dawns and the day star arises in the heart," like the sudden sunburst of an Oriental morning. So Methodism has taught. *Does* Christ "prolong his days" and come home to human hearts, or has He merely left us the legacy of His influence in the exemplary figure pictured in the stained glass windows of the Gospels? He "whose goings forth are from of old, from everlasting," appeared visibly on the stage of history for a few years, and He still goes forth conquering and to conquer. He walks the roads of today as He walked the Emmaus road of yesterday, making the hearts of men burn within them as He communes with them. He is "alive forevermore" and comes nearer to those who trust Him than He did to the Bethany family of old; nearer than He came to the disciples when He washed their feet; nearer than

He came to John when that beloved disciple leaned on His breast. "Closer is he than breathing and nearer than hands and feet." The desire often expressed to have lived in the days of His manifestation in the flesh betrays spiritual blindness.

But wherefore this dream of the earthly abode,
Of Humanity clothed in the brightness of God?
Were my spirit but turned from the outward and dim
I could gaze, even now, on the presence of Him.

Oh, the outward hath gone! but in glory and power,
The Spirit surviveth the things of an hour;
Unchanged, undecaying, His Pentecost flame
On the heart's secret altar is burning the same.
—John Greenleaf Whittier

True believers furnish perpetual proof that Christ is risen from the dead because He lives in and through them. Nominal professors who deny the possibility of knowing Him in His intimate indwelling remand Him to the tomb and roll the stone across the door. All of the admiring words with which they magnify Him as a historical character are only sweet spices in which they embalm a dead Christ.

Jesus "showed himself alive after his passion by many infallible proofs," and Paul, in I Cor. 15:8 includes himself among the witnesses that Christ has risen, by saying, "He was seen of me also, as of one born out of due time." John possessed indisputable evidence of the reality of the Incarnate Christ. By the senses of hearing, sight and touch, he had experienced outward fellowship with the personal Word of Life. Leaning on Jesus' breast and listening to the whispered secrets of the Eternal, he received his B. D. (Beloved Disciple) degree, but the conclusion of the incarnate manifestation did not mean graduation from the school of Christ. It was preliminary to a continued and fuller revelation. "Truly (said John) our fellowship *is* (and not only *was*) with the Father and with his Son, Jesus Christ." The contact, so far from being broken, had become more intimate under purely spiritual conditions. And it is not an apostolic monopoly. It was John's desire, as he declared in his First Epistle "that ye also may have fellowship with us."

The Holy Land is not Palestine. We stand on holy ground when we face Christ. Jesus said to his disciples, "I will not leave you comfortless: I will come to you," literally, "I will not leave you orphans." The church that rejects or ignores the Holy Ghost has not the Elder Brother, for the Holy Ghost alone reveals and glorifies Him, and the church that has not the Elder Brother has not the heavenly Father, for the Father is revealed and honored by the Son, and what should have been a joyful household of faith is an unhappy orphanage. "I will come to you," is the promise to all who believe.

But what shall be the manner of His coming to the individual? That is determined by the nature of man's deepest need. Man has broken the law, and the law makes no provision for the forgiveness of its violators. It has but one consistent counterpart, and that is penalty. Man is guilty and doomed under its merciless glare. "But," said Bishop R. S. Foster, "the probation under law is not final. The case is transferred from the law to the gospel. Probation has been carried over from the region of law to the provisions of grace. It is God who changed the venue and ordered the trial to proceed under new conditions." That was not done by ignoring or abrogating law. Christ honored the law in His substitutionary atonement, and now becomes the Advocate of penitent sinners in the divinely established court of grace. When pardon is granted there the intelligence is conveyed to the contrite heart by the witness of the Spirit. Instantly the burden is lifted, the sting of guilt is extracted, fears are dissipated, and peace prevails. The holy Judge is seen as the heavenly Father and the pardoned prodigal feels at home in His presence. That "felt" experience of forgiveness and reconciliation takes the whole matter of personal salvation out of the realm of conjecture. The night of doubt is succeeded by the day of certainty.

> We cannot doubt, when once the ear of listening faith
>   has heard,
> With all-responsive thrill of love, the music of his word!
> He gives the witness that excels all argument or sign—
> When we have heard it for ourselves we *know* it is divine!
>
> And then, oh, then, the wail is stilled, the wandering
>   is o'er,
> The rest is gained, the certainty that wavers nevermore;
> And then the full, unquivering praise arises glad and
>   strong,
> And life becomes the prelude of the everlasting song!
>   —*Frances Ridley Havergal*

Coincident, and vitally connected with the change of legal status in justification, is the renewal of the nature in regeneration. The believer is born again, and "God sends forth the

Spirit of His Son into the heart crying, Abba Father." The lips could have articulated the words in the poor clumsy language of earth before, but the heart would have remained dumb. The inability of the Ephraimites to pronounce Shibboleth at the fords of Jordan suggests, if one may depart from the conventional interpretation, that a difference in pronunciation may indicate a difference in family, in nationality, in culture. The once-born always stumble in their speech when they attempt to imitate the language of the children of the Kingdom, however much they may drill themselves in the evangelical terminology. There are words in the vocabulary of faith on which they choke. "No man can say that Jesus is Lord but by the Holy Ghost," however smoothly he may call Him Teacher. Only the twice-born can utter the inimitable "accent of the Holy Ghost," with its spontaneity and note of reality. The well-instructed theologian might furnish a correct map of the kingdom of God on the basis of Bible descriptions, and talk about it in the coldest, abstract manner, while the humblest Christian as a "fellow-citizen with the saints and of the household of God" joyfully explores his inheritance that is more real to him than the earth on which he stands.

> "Think not the faith by which the just shall live
>   Is a dead creed, a map correct of heaven,
> Much less a feeling fond and fugitive,
>   A thoughtless gift withdrawn as soon as given;
> It is the affirmation and the act
>   That bids eternal truth be present fact."
>
> —Hartley Coleridge

An unbridged chasm lies between those who *know* and

105

those who know not. Bare intellectual assent pays respectful tribute to the truth and still leaves one a full member of "the synagogue of Satan," for "devils also believe and tremble"; but trustful committal of the heart to the operation of the Spirit transforms the nature and brings one into conscious membership in "the church of the first born which are written in heaven." Immediately the genius of the communion of saints is understood as if by intuition. All the deep affinities of the soul are with "the royal priesthood, the holy nation, the peculiar people" of highest birth. Where men have obtained "like precious faith" with all the sons of God, there is mutual recognition and understanding, and "a stranger doth not intermeddle with their joy" since he is not to the manner born. "Eye hath not seen, nor ear heard, neither have entered into the heart of man, the things which God hath prepared for them that love him. But God hath revealed them unto us by his Spirit." I Cor. 2:9, 10.

Beyond regeneration and distinct from it, but not detached from it, is entire sanctification, in answer to the cry "Finish then thy new creation, pure and spotless let us be." "If we walk in the light as he is in the light we have fellowship one with another" and we shall walk into the "fullness of the blessing of the gospel of Christ," "the blood of Jesus Christ God's Son cleansing us from all sin." Bunyan's Beulah Land is on the road to the Heavenly City. Its citizens are called "The holy people." From its heights "Doubting Castle" cannot so much as be seen. It is the land of perfect moral health. Its inhabitants never say, "I am sick." Regeneration communicates the new life. Entire sanctification cleanses away the remains of the old life, the disease of inbred sin. And who would object to perfect health in body or spirit?

106

Health could be stigmatized as abnormal only by the victims of a disease that cripples the reason. The exuberance of health could be branded as fanaticism only by those afflicted with spiritual low blood pressure. The clear vision of the "pure in heart" could be mistaken for the visionary only by those who have never experienced the anointing of the eyes with "the eye salve" of which Jesus spoke to John.

Thousands have been so certain about these matters that they have suffered the loss of all things to maintain their testimony. The martyrs did not gamble their all on a guess; their faith was "the substance of things hoped for, the evidence of things not seen." Phantoms do not cheer in the midst of torments. The suffering saints of old "took joyfully the spoiling of their goods, *knowing* that in heaven they had a better and enduring *substance*," and they knew it because they had some of the "substance" in hand, in the "earnest of the inheritance," the down payment in kind, the allowance from home. Whatever might happen to one of those who "dwelt in the secret place of the most high," and "tasted the good word of God, and of the powers of the world to come," he could never doubt or forget the wondrous experience.

Aye, tho' thou then shouldst strike him from his glory,
Blind and tormented, maddened and alone,
Even on the cross would he maintain his story,
Yes, and in hell would whisper, "I have known."
                                        —F. W. H. Myers

III. There is precious truth in an eternal code to be preserved in practice.

Wesley said of the moral law that it is "an incorruptible

picture of the High and Holy One that inhabiteth eternity—
the original ideas of truth and good, which were lodged in
the uncreated mind from eternity, now drawn forth and
clothed with such a vehicle as to appear even to human
understanding—a copy of the eternal mind, a transcript
of the divine nature—the fairest offspring of the everlasting
Father, the brightest efflux of His essential wisdom, the
visible beauty of the Most High. It is the delight and
wonder of cherubim and seraphim, and all the company of
heaven, and the glory and joy of every wise believer, every
well-instructed child of God upon earth."

The child of God delights in the law of God, and his
obedient conduct proves it. Doctrine is the root of the tree;
experience is the trunk of the tree, filled with vital sap; conduct is the flower and fruit of the tree, adorning the doctrine
and glorifying the experience. God writes the law in the
heart and the believer copies it in the life.

If we might revert to Forsyth's statement that "we may
see but a partial cross," it reminds us that many who profess to acknowledge Christ as Savior on the cross, have torn
from the cross the superscription that proclaims Him King
(not the superscription placed there by Pilate, but the one
placed there by the Supreme Law-giver who said, "I have
set my King upon my holy hill of Zion.") They would exploit
His love while flouting His law. They would be redeemed
from sin but not redeemed *unto* God. They would trust Him
as "a lamb as it had been slain," but they would not obey
Him as the Lamb "in the midst of the throne." They will
have Christ as Lover but not as Lord; they will have Him as
Propitiation but not as Potentate.

But the cross cannot be split and Christ cannot be divided.

If Christ lifts us from the horrible pit He must lead us in paths of righteousness and "establish our goings."

The unregenerate man who says, "To follow the golden rule is sufficient," should be reminded that a materialistic philosopher recognized the impossibility of getting golden conduct out of leaden instincts. The declaration, "The Sermon on the Mount is enough for me," is flippantly made by those who have not struck the first note in the "Heavenly Octave" of the Beatitudes, with which it begins. How can they run the whole gamut of infinite music there when they have not even sounded the "deep bass of penitence" involved in its prelude requiring poverty of spirit and mourning for sin? Only the new creature can sing the new song and walk in newness of life. Not by observing a scientifically formulated dietetic regimen, not by relieving pressure on the brain, not by supplying the needs of an "undernourished endocrine gland" is holy living secured, for the seat of our trouble is deeper than the body. Nor can good living be secured by faultless ethical teaching, because the mind is a part of the field of sinful symptoms. The cause of wrongdoing is in a depth beyond the mind. "Out of the heart of man proceed evil thoughts" and all the unholy brood of associated sins. "A new heart and a new spirit" make it natural for us to "live soberly, and righteously, and godly in this present world."

Righteous living is inspired by spontaneous impulses in the redeemed nature, but it is not an automatic result. Thomas Huxley said, "I protest that if some great power would agree to make me always think what is true and do what is right, on condition of being turned into a sort of clock and wound up every morning, I should instantly close with the offer."

But a moral automaton is a contradiction in terms. Regeneration does not transform personality into a machine with a good supply of oil provided in entire sanctification to assure its frictionless operation. After the love of God is shed abroad in the heart, the affections joyfully cry, "Thy will be done," but the will of man must make repeated choices at the points where the road forks and the mind is perplexed to know what the will of God is.

Then arises the necessity for the patient, careful search for light. When the light shines it is the business of the illuminated person to "bring the bottom of his life up to the top of his light," to use the words of an old Puritan. "As for God, his work is perfect," and the heart is thoroughly cleansed by the baptism of the Spirit. But as for man his work is imperfect because he is finite, and the effort he makes to conform his deportment to all the inward impulses and principles of holiness will be progressively successful as knowledge and grace increase. Wesley taught that great love does not necessarily imply great light. So one may have faultless intentions in a pure heart, but not be faultless in action. As the young Christian grows in grace and knowledge, many things which did not appear to be sinful before are eliminated as not seeming to be altogether in character for a Christian. To others these things might seem innocent enough, but under increased light he detects the dangers that lurk in them.

Both purification and suppression have place in the man who desires to work out by faithfulness the thing that has been worked in him by faith. The carnal element must be extirpated and the purely human element regulated. That which is no essential part of man's nature as God made him must be cleansed away, and that which is God's original handiwork in man must be controlled in a world where sin abounds. After sin has been killed by divine execution something remains to be curbed by the will of man divinely aided. The Apostle James compares this control to putting bits in the horse's mouth with which to restrain and guide him. It is no partial control that is exercised by the Christian, for James more than hints that if a man is able to bridle his tongue he will be able to bridle the whole body. The natural powers are domesticated by grace, and the responsibility is placed upon us of harnessing those powers and holding a regulative rein on them, so they may be hitched to the divine purpose. High, Christian living is achieved by the watchful and firm hold upon the reins, directing our actions to the glory of God.

To cast off the bridle is, of course, to sin against God, but the reins may be slackened in a moment of almost inadvertent carelessness in times of relaxation and diversion, and grave harm be done to those who are watching and listening for any inconsistency. Emerson said, "Your behavior is always under examination by committees little suspected, a police in citizen's clothes, who are awarding or denying you very high prizes when you least think of it." Much fine preaching has been neutralized by those who failed to keep the mouth with a bridle when the wicked were before them. Many a first-class love feast has been dissipated soon after its close by a second-class gab-fest poisoned with gossip. Many a prayer meeting in which a man has blessed God has been nullified by the man's going out to curse a fellow man if only with "faint praise." Paying lip tribute to a holy code of law has no influence, except a bad one, unless it is translated into a holy mode of life. High profession coupled with low practice sounds a destructive discord in the world.

It goes almost without saying that on the border line of doubtful practices the true Christian will give God and his conscience the benefit of the doubt. Those who are repeatedly skirting the outermost boundary of the lawful are in danger of moving by a very short step into unlawful territory. But it is a finer point of Christian ethics to restrain one's self from ranging freely in the field of the lawful when such action is open to misinterpretation by those of weak conscience, and it becomes an occasion of stumbling to them. Paul declared, "All things are lawful for me, but all things edify not," and if they do not edify or build up they may tear down. So the Pauline verdict is, "If meat make my brother to offend (or stumble) I will eat no flesh while the world standeth." The possibility of destroying with my legitimate meat one for whom Christ died is a matter for most serious consideration. This point needs wise guarding, however. The impossible task is not laid upon us of conforming to the whims of every person who undertakes to lord it over our conscience. It is the interest of the *weak* brother, with his manifold infirmities that we are tenderly to regard, and not the dictatorial demands of the *strong* critic.

Christian conduct also has a self-ward bearing. There are reflex benefits accruing to the actor. As he exercises himself unto godliness, the principles and virtues involved in such exercise are developed and strengthened just as the muscles of the body are developed by exercise. The inward life grows by outward expression. The character also takes on a fineness of texture as the soul attends to the more delicate shadings of conduct in the etiquette of holiness. Pharisaical scrupulosity on microscopic nonessentials is infinitely below the extreme carefulness without strain that comes to grace the character of the man who sincerely endeavors to walk worthy of the Lord unto all pleasing.

Conduct also has a God-ward bearing. The honor of the Divine Name is at stake. God's religion is on trial in the world. Christian men and women are witnesses for the defense. If the walk of the professor belies his talk, the religion he represents is discredited and God is blasphemed because of him. The purpose of all the high privileges to which we are called is that we may "show forth the praises (or virtues) of him who hath called us out of darkness into his marvelous light." If in waiting upon the Lord we renew our strength so that in a rapture of love and joy we mount up with wings as eagles, it is to fit us to come down again and run the way of God's commandments without wearying, and follow the dusty, monotonous road of everyday life, with patient, persistent plodding, without fainting. Such men are a royal diadem in the hand of God with which He crowns Himself in honor. God rejoices over them and delights to hold them up to inspection, asking the prince of this world and all his little human princelings as He did in the day of Job, "Hast thou considered my servant."

The practice of true religion cannot be preserved except as we propagate true religion. The Holy Spirit who has His home in our hearts is ever prompting and leading us to communicate the gospel sacrificially in preaching and witnessing. One of Mark Guy Pearse's parables portrays this truth fascinatingly. "It was in the early springtime that a certain man went forth to get him a packet of flower seeds. They were wrapped in a paper gay with pictured flowers, vivid scarlet and green leaved, and tied with a silken string. On the paper was a label and thereon the name of the seed in stately Latin, not quite correct, but solemn, 'Lilium Ecclesiasticum Methodisticum.' He took them home with him, and set them delicately in a cupboard on which were designs elegantly carved—angels hovered, and saints with halos walked as in a garden of Eden. Then the seeds talked together. 'We ought to be very thankful to enjoy such sacred privileges. So fine and costly a cupboard for our resting place, rich in its dainty symbolism. And a name proclaiming our orthodoxy in Latin so learned and distinguished.' Hear what happened. The mildew came upon them and they rotted. But another packet of seed was there that cried—'What care we for gay wrappers and silken strings! What to us is your costly cupboard and orthodox label! Fling us forth into the earth, out there where the bleak winds blow, and the rains beat. Bury us that we may live.' And later stood the flower to bless the world with beauty and fragrance and gladness. The seed that kept itself to itself rotted. The seed that gave itself away found itself in a flower." Seed is not for hoarding. It is for scattering and germination and multiplication. The "precious truth" of the text is the "precious seed" of Psalm 126 that we are to bear forth and sow, watering it with our tears, in the fullest assurance that we shall have the joy of harvesting many sheaves that will furnish more seed for the sower and bread for the eater.

This has been the method of Free Methodism wherever she has been true to her holy Methodist traditions. May we never indulge in the miser's boast about the spiritual wealth that has been placed in our hands, but rather let us make heavy investments of the treasure entrusted to us and enlarge the business of world evangelization until our work is done and the junior partners in the firm take our places and continue the dedicated succession until all the results are gathered up at the sunset of earth's day and brought into the everlasting kingdom of Jesus Christ to enrich it forever.

Chapter 6

THE HERITAGE TRANSMITTED

It is necessary in considering a subject of such magnitude as this to take the highest ground at the outset. Only from an elevated position can we see into the distance and recognize the importance of our relation to the future of the church. A character in Goethe's *Faust* said,

"What dazzles, for the Moment spends its spirit:
What's genuine, shall Posterity inherit,"

and a buffoon replied,

"Posterity! Don't name the word to me!
If *I* should choose to preach Posterity,
Where would you get contemporary fun?"

Beginning at such a low level of self-indulgence everything is seen in the light of human littleness. The self-centered soul "contracts his firmament to the compass of a tent," to use Emerson's language, and he has no heavenly firmament above him, and no landscape stretching out before him to far horizons. Churches are in danger of bogging down in this low-lying plain where "contemporary fun" or contemporary excitement, or contemporary comfort become paramount. Such churches can have no spiritual progeny. They end in human futility.

If we take the highest ground and begin with a great premise we shall arrive at great conclusions, especially if

117

the premise postulates an infinitely great Person as the originating cause of an endless line of life. Let the writer of the 145th Psalm state the premise, "Great is the Lord, and greatly to be praised; and his greatness is unsearchable." Then hear his conclusion, "One generation shall praise thy works to another, and shall declare thy mighty acts."

I. In the Psalmist's premise I find my credo which underlies all my hopes for the future of the church.

1. I believe in the perpetuity of the divine action. God is. God only is great. God is here. "In him we live and move and have our being." God is in action. He "worketh hitherto." The world is not self-propelled and self-sustained. Mother Nature, to whom the unregenerate attribute everything, is as fictional as Mother Hubbard.

Blessed are those who can sense the presence and the goings of God in His world and are sure He never leaves on a vacation and never slumbers or sleeps. Enswathed everywhere by Him, they do not miss Him as the poet represented the fishes as missing the sea with which they were surrounded and in which they were submerged.

> "Oh, where is the sea?" the fishes cried,
>   As they swam the Atlantic waters through;
>   We've heard of the sea and the ocean tide
>   And we long to gaze on its waters blue."

The believer not only *feels* after God; he *finds* Him everywhere. To him "the God of glory thundereth." The stormy wind fulfills His word. He sendeth out his lightning. "The Lord sitteth upon the flood." "He maketh *his* sun to rise on the evil and on the good, and sendeth rain on the just and on the unjust." "He clothes the grass of the field" with beauty surpassing Solomon's glory. "He openeth his hand and satisfieth the desire of every living thing." We recognize our blessings as more than accidental windfalls. They are hand picked.

We believe in a God who governs in a providential order. As the writer of our Psalm says, "(His) kingdom is an everlasting kingdom, and (His) dominion endureth throughout all generations." Things are not staggering blindly on. The secular historian may see the events of history as so many loose threads dangling or tangling in an unintelligent universe, but men of faith see the outlines of a pattern in a fabric that constitutes the historical handiwork of God. All things are working together for good to His kingdom. The black keys of His justice and the white keys of His mercy are sounding out one music. He can gird a Cyrus who does not know Him and make him the servant of the divine purpose. Atilla, the Hun, was called "the scourge of God," and times without number God has used godless nations to scourge and discipline nations that once were godly but had come to forget Him, and then has thrown the scourge into the scrap heap of history. Thus He maketh the wrath of man to praise Him.

Frequently God works in judgment and men see "the might of his terrible acts" referred to in the sixth verse of our Psalm. P. T. Forsyth said, "The course of historic events is that of a series of judgments, each like an automatic release when the cup of iniquity was filled." And a great poet wrote,

"Backward look across the ages and the beacon moments
    see,

> That, like peaks of some sunk continent, jut through
>   Oblivion's sea;
> Not an ear in court or market for the low foreboding cry
> Of those Crises, God's stern winnowers, from whose feet
>   earth's chaff must fly;
> Never shows the choice momentous till the judgment
>   hath passed by.
> "Careless seems the great Avenger; history's pages but
>   record
> One death-grapple in the darkness 'twixt old systems and
>   the word;
> Truth forever on the scaffold, Wrong forever on the
>   throne
> Yet that scaffold sways the future, and behind the dim
>   unknown,
> Standeth God within the shadow, keeping watch above
>   his own."—James Russell Lowell

The greatest things that happen in this world completely escape the scrutiny of the news-hawks. They can report the shadow, but not the God within the shadow and the purpose of His judgments. They can see the mystery of history, but they cannot see the divine mastery of history.

Woven into the whole web of time is God's redeeming purpose. There would have been no history had it not been for God's purpose to redeem man. The creation and perpetuation of the race are justified by the purpose to redeem. "In the fulness of time" the eternal purpose of God took visible form in the incarnation of His Son. He got into our humanity without our invitation or consent. And, as has been said, the greatest thing ever done *for* us was done

120

behind our backs. It was while our backs were turned to God that Christ died for us. And to make the atonement effective the Spirit has come to reprove the world of sin and to take the things of Christ and show them to believers. So God is here in abiding gracious action.

2. I believe in the perpetuity of man's nature and need, and therefore in the perpetual promise of a response by man to the revelation of God. "Man is very permanent in what most makes him man," it has been said. He has an ineradicable moral nature. He distinguishes between good and evil. He chooses the evil. But while he embraces vice he admires virtue at a distance. He will defend his wickedness openly and then hate and lash himself for it secretly. The truth commends itself to his conscience while his passions resent its demands.

Man was created in the Divine Image and nothing below him matches and meets his need. The very madness of man's pursuit of pleasure in our time is evidence that he has not found what he craves. The best the world can give him is empty husks, highly seasoned, and washed down by the heady wine of moral intoxication that buries his misery in temporary oblivion. He cannot fill his empty heart with the empty husks of pleasure. It is the sheerest nonsense to say that communism is filling up the yawning vacuum in modern life. If communism could create the Mohammedan paradise of plenty that it promises, it would no more feed the heart of man than the east wind feeds the body. When men come to themselves they cry like orphans for a heavenly Father and the provision of the Father's house.

3. I believe in the perpetuity of the church and her perpetual success. Oliver Wendell Holmes tells of a boy who

deflated his little brother's toy balloon by pricking it with a pin. That night the father stood at a window with the little fellow, looking at the moon, and the boy whispered, "Do not show it to brother. He will stick a pin in it." Many a toy balloon filled with a few puffs of human breath, insubstantial theories, have been deflated by the sharp points of criticism, and not a few have become terrified, thinking it spelled the doom of the Church. But, she still "goes forth as the morning, fair as the moon, clear as the sun, and terrible as an army with banners."

> "Crowns and thrones may perish,
>   Kingdoms rise and wane,
> But the church of Jesus
>   Constant will remain;
> Gates of hell can never
>   'Gainst the church prevail;
> We have Christ's own promise,
>   And that cannot fail."

I would liken the Spirit's movement in the world, of which the church is an integral part, to the world's greatest river, the Gulf Stream, which comes from the tropical region north of the Equator, pushing its warm water through the cold Atlantic for many hundreds of miles, a river in the sea, ninety-five miles wide, a mile deep, and with a volume equal to hundreds of Mississippis, keeping its distinctive color, challenging the icy cold of the North, creating a climate favorable to growth and fruitfulness, where otherwise frigid death would reign. It has maintained its course through long centuries. So the church has moved in the God-appointed channel with the movement of the Spirit, "from age to age the same," and has changed the world's moral climate. This heavenly Gulf Stream has survived raging storms of persecution that sometimes lashed it for many years. All the mad power of Rome could not deflect the current. The storms of persecution were furious in the early days of Methodism but the current of life won the day and transformed England. Hurricanes of unbelief with the imposing names Deism, Rationalism, Free Thought, and Humanism have borne down upon the current without bending or breaking it. The troubled sea of human life casting up the mire of vice and the dirt of materialism has beaten against it without befouling it. The tidal waves of Communism will never master it. The church will continue serenely and triumphantly on her way, and He that sitteth in the heavens will ever laugh at the puny human forces that combine to oppose her.

After having stated my certainty about the future of the church of Christ in this optimistic credo, I wish
II. To express my sober concern in the light of the Psalmist's conclusion, "One generation shall praise thy works to another."

The holy seed will always exist. My concern is that we shall ever be a part of that unbroken lineage that produces a holy seed. The saintly succession will not fail. It is my concern that we do not fail the saintly succession. The witness will never die. My concern is that we may never fail to voice it. The Gulf Stream of the church of the Spirit will flow in full volume and resistless power to the end of time, but my concern is that we stay in the Stream. It was a small craft our fathers launched into this Stream a century ago. It is still a small boat, comparatively, but I prefer a small sailboat *in* the Stream driven by the trade winds of God, to a large luxury liner *out* of the Stream.

While avoiding sectarian narrowness, we should not become so fearful of seeming to be sectarian that our charity degenerates into a latitudinarian spirit which submerges everything distinctive in the gospel, and swallows almost everything else that carries the Christian name. This brings to mind what George Cookman once said in a speech:

"It was announced some years ago that old Bigotry was dead and fairly buried. I am sorry to be under the necessity of informing this audience that it has been discovered of late that he left behind him an only child—a prodigal son, who is arrived at man's estate. This son is known by the name of Liberalism. Young Liberalism is the very antipodes of his old father. He is handsome, polite, insinuating—and, although somewhat superficial, possesses that polish and tact which impose upon general observers. He speaks all languages, subscribes to all creeds, holds a levee with all sects and parties, is friendly with everybody, but stands identified with nobody. He professes to abhor religious controversy, and disposes of all doctrinal questions by a motion of indefinite postponement. He can swallow the wafer with the Papist, receive the cup with the Protestant, and thrust the Westminster Confession and the Methodist Discipline into the same pocket. You can never find Liberalism at home, or, rather 'he is never at home but when from home.' He sails all waters under all colors; he exhibits the papers of all nations, but he hails to no port, he charters to no country, and, therefore, we strongly suspect that he is, in reality, a *pirate*."

The tolerant religious liberalism of our day (here I am not using the word liberalism in the theological sense) has gone to the extreme of taking in Roman Catholicism with all its intolerance. When it was first suggested that the Panama Canal be built, it is said that the project was severely criticized in Europe. The French particularly expressed the fear that such a canal would divert the waters of the Equatorial Current into the Pacific and there would be no Gulf Stream to keep Europe from becoming unbearably frigid. What the French foolishly feared the Romish church has foolishly attempted in the religious world. She has constructed her canal, and declared that the Gulf Stream of spiritual life flows through it exclusively. With ponderous ecclesiastical machinery she operates the locks and lets all comers through for a price. She represents a pagan apostasy hundreds of years old. She left the Stream early in church history. Let us avoid the breadth that runs to shallowness and involves what Bishop Pearce called "the devil's charity."

Our craft *cannot* be driven from the Stream but it *could* drift from the Stream. There are subtle cross currents that could almost insensibly bear us from our course unless we keep a sharp lookout.

There are sparkling currents of intellectualism that sweep athwart our course. "Ye shall be as gods, knowing," was Satan's first promise and man's believing it was his first and worst peril. Intellect is good when it is subordinated to the God-illumined heart and recognizes its own limitations. It is the deification of intellect we have to fear. The intellectual is too frequently dominated by the spirit of doubt and denial. Because he cannot think his way into spiritual reality

125

he denies the existence of spiritual reality. **Men of**

> "Athenian intelligence
> But of man's tragic guilt no sense
> To holiness acutely dense"

have become the educators of the people. Altars to the unknown god are erected in every major seat of secular learning in America. To men with bright brains and blind hearts spiritual things will always be foolishness, and their only tribute to the spiritual order will be clever witticisms and polite sneers. If we keep our vision clear we shall ever be reminding ourselves that these things are "hid from the wise and prudent and revealed unto babes."

When the intellectualist uses the jargon of modern psychology he imagines he has explained all so-called spiritual phenomena on natural grounds. G. A. Studdert-Kennedy of England described the probings of personality by the psychologist in this way,

> "He takes the saints to pieces,
>   And labels all the parts,
> He tabulates the secrets
>   Of loyal, loving hearts.
> He probes their selfless passion
>   And knows exactly why
> The martyr goes out singing
>   To suffer and to die.
> The beatific vision
>   That brings them to their knees
> He smilingly reduces
>   To infant fantasies.

The Freudian unconscious
   Quite easily explains
The splendor of their sorrows
   The pageant of their pains.
The manifold temptations
   Wherewith the flesh can vex
The saintly soul, are samples
   Of Oedipus complex.
The subtle sex perversion
   His eagle glance can tell,
That makes their joyous heaven
   The horror of their hell.
His reasoning is perfect,
   His proofs as plain as paint,
He has but one small weakness,
   He cannot make a saint."

We are in the saint-making business and we cannot allow any psychological theories of the hour to divert us from the central task. Pastoral psychiatry, while useful in its restricted sphere, should, with us, always be a poor second to the spiritual approaches and methods that have been effective since the days of the apostles in solving the basic problems of humanity.

We should know the thought movements of our day but we should *correct them* and not let them *capture us*. It is more than pathetic to see churches waiting almost breathlessly for the thinkers of the world to make the motion on some subject, and then with unholy haste second the motion so they may be abreast of the times, only to be deeply chagrined when the thinkers move a re-consideration of the

127

subject, and then move so many modifying amendments that they and the churches are left in complete bewilderment.

From the beginning, the Free Methodist Church has believed in Christian education, but if she ever minifies the adjective and magnifies the noun so she may keep in the scholastic swim she will drift from her course. She may carry many high-sounding titles fore and many dignified degrees aft, and be tempted to go by intellectual dead reckoning. If she yields to the temptation she will flounder in the shallows of the prevailing religious philosophy or crash against the icebergs of formality as many an ecclesiastical Titanic has in the past.

"Every wind of doctrine" sweeps back and forth across the great Gulf Stream of historic Christianity and every church catches at least some of the spray from the pretentious waves of speculation that are set in motion in the name of fundamental truth. Many are all agog over the identification of God and Magog and where they will grapple in mortal conflict, while the battle between the God of heaven and the god of this world rages about them, and they are as serenely indifferent as if it matters not which side they espouse. Others are intensely interested in the question as to who the ultimate Antichrist will be while daily the many antichrists deny the deity of our Lord from press and pulpit. Still others are agitated over the question of whether or not the saints will go through the great tribulation, and the writer knows of a church that was split over the question, when all concerned should have been interested primarily in the declaration of the Word that we must through much tribulation enter the kingdom of God and should have

128

strengthened one another in the struggle. Men have exhibited intense earnestness in contending for a particular mode of the rite of water baptism when they were cool toward any proclamation of a righteousness established by the baptism of the Spirit.

The central Stream has been struck times without number by proud waves of fanatical notions with scraps of Scripture floating on the surface, and unstable souls have been swept by them from the deck of more than one denominational craft. But it is our task to stay in the current and take for our chart the whole of the divine revelation in the Bible so we may keep on an even keel and be always certain of our spiritual latitude and longitude.

Time would fail us to point out in any thorough way the cross currents of deterministic theologies that could fittingly adopt Omar Khayyam's conception of men as the

"helpless Pieces of the Game (God) plays
Upon this Chequer-board of Nights and Days,"

of movements with high spiritual pretensions that are breeders of low morals, "raging waves of the sea, foaming out their own shame," as Jude described certain religionists of his day, of currents that carry the light chaff of the religious world into the pulpit, making the preacher a clown, and into the pew, making the singing an echo of tin-pan alley, and movements that major on the microscopic, raising a huge clamor over perfectly indifferent matters, like an

"ocean into tempest wrought
To waft a feather or to drown a fly,"

129

and are none the better for floating the feather of a fancied virtue or drowning the fly of a fancied evil, and of mongrel movements that attempt to mix certain elements of doctrinal conservatism with certain elements of doctrinal liberalism.

But perhaps the cross curents are not the greatest threat to the church that seriously desires to stay in the central Stream, for their very contradiction of the things that are deepest in her convictions and highest in her esteem will alert her to the danger. The parallel currents that seem so much in harmony with what we believe may tempt us to leave the Gulf Stream. That is an immense peril. Here is a large current that is legally correct and doctrinally sound. It fits the main Current, but it is dreadfully cold. For years, John Wesley plied the oars of his little canoe striving for personal salvation in this cold current. He was a laborious religionist, the finest kind of legalist, as was Saul of Tarsus before he met Jesus on the Damascus road. One day Wesley got his bearings and moved into the warm Gulf Stream. Then he witnessed, "I felt my heart strangely warmed." From that moment, the man who said that naturally he would much rather be "a saunterer in academic shades" than be an itinerant preacher, impelled by the warm heart, took to the road and sounded the message of an uttermost salvation across England, Ireland, Scotland and Wales, kindling fires that burn to this day. A movement may claim to be evangelical without being evangelistic because it does not believe in a heart religion that gives the assurance which is indispensable to glad witnessing.

Let us not move a hair's breadth from our position because larger vessels than ours are plowing the cold waters of a lifeless orthodoxy. Keep in mind that God has always worked through mighty minorities. If the warmth of our devotion incites the cold-hearted to stigmatize us as fanatics, let us not be so much concerned that we shall attempt to lower the temperature in order to be on good terms with the cold majority. Our great adversary would rather cool us off than kill us off.

All of which leads me to say that we can only propagate and perpetuate what we have preserved as a living reality. We can transmit only what we have. We have inherited a wonderful tradition and a mighty history of holy influence. We must not ignore or belittle the past. We may well look at it and learn from it. But we dare not idolize it or try to live on it. I would adapt some lines of James Russell Lowell, with one or two slight changes, to the thought of our possibilities and perils at this stage of the voyage.

" 'Tis as easy to be heroes as to sit the idle slaves
Of a legendary virtue carved upon our fathers' graves,
Worshippers of light ancestral make the present light a
    crime;—
Was (our) Mayflower launched by cowards, steered by
    men behind their time?
Turn those tracks toward Past or Future, that make
    (Pekin so) sublime?
They were men of present valor, stalwart old iconoclasts,
Unconvinced by axe and gibbet that all virtue was the
    Past's;
But we make their truth our falsehood, thinking that
    hath made us free,

Hoarding it in mouldy parchments, while our tender
spirits flee

The (strong) grasp of that great Impulse which drove
them across the sea."

If we stay in the Stream we shall always be in the grasp
of that strong Impulse which drove our fathers across the
sea of their generation, and we shall be makers of heroic
history.

If we stay in the Stream which is "a pure river of water of
life," we shall always feel its purifying power, and will
propagate the gospel of heart purity. If we leave the Stream
we shall lose the cleansing, and once the experienced reality
of heart holiness is gone, what Wesley termed "the grand
depositum lodged with the people called Methodists," the
priceless treasure of holiness truth, will be cast overboard
as so much excess baggage, and our mission will have been
repudiated and ended.

If we stay in the Stream we shall sail under orders. The
law of God "holy, just and good" will be our rule of conduct.
We shall so delight in the law of the Lord that the spirit of
Deut. 6:5, 9 will be beautifully fulfilled in us. "Thou shalt
love the Lord thy God with all thine heart, and with all thy
soul, and with all thy might. And these words, which I
command thee this day, shall be in thine heart: And thou
shalt teach them diligently unto thy children, and shalt talk
of them when thou sittest in thine house, and when thou
walkest by the way, and when thou liest down, and when
thou risest up. And thou shalt bind them for a sign upon
thine hand, and they shall be as frontlets between thine eyes.
And thou shalt write them upon the posts of thy house,

and on thy gates." The law of God written in the heart will have many carbon copies in the life, and those who live soberly and righteously and godly in this world will be living epistles read and known of all men. It is our responsibility and privilege to give the world an up-to-date translation of the holy law in holy conduct. When we do that our practice amplifies rather than muffles our profession and as we thus echo God we shall be heard around the world.

If we stay in the Stream we shall continue while in the world to be separated from the spirit of the world, for the Stream will never mingle with the world-ocean through which it flows to lose its distinctiveness in a worldly churchliness and a churchly worldliness. We have our own atmosphere of superior joy and peace and the world can add nothing to it. Vanity Fair would be bankrupted if it depended on us. We can walk through it without making a purchase though we are branded as fools. Let the spirit of the age be what it will, our mission is to maintain the spirit of the eternal, remembering what a Church of England clergyman said, "The Church which marries the spirit of the age will be left a widow in the next generation." It is not inevitable that any church forget its calling to be part of "a chosen generation, a royal priesthood, an holy nation, a peculiar people, showing forth the excellencies of him who hath called us out of darkness into his marvelous light," and drift into the deadly atmosphere of the world. But it might be a warning to any church, our own included, seriously to recall words quoted with approval by so great a scholar and saint as Archbishop Trench from the writings of a man who did much to prepare the way for the Reformation. "The first generation will be holy, the second learned, the third worldly." Despite this somber prognostication, the holy church *may* remain holy, and draw into its shining wake many a disillusioned devotee of the world.

If we stay in the Stream we shall keep the unity of the Spirit, in whose life of love we live, and our witness will be perpetuated. Wesley said, "What can hurt the Methodists so called but the Methodists? Only let them not fight one another, and 'no weapon formed against them shall prosper.'" Whether we be commanding officers, petty officers, or privates on this man-of-war called the Church, if we "love one another with a pure heart fervently," victory is assured. Only mutiny aboard can destroy the ship and compel us to surrender.

If we stay in the Stream, which is crimson with sacrificial love, since it proceeds from the throne of God and the Lamb, a Lamb as it had been slain, we shall share in the spiritual sovereignty that always springs out of sacrifice. The treasure committed to us can be transmitted successfully only by the nail-pierced hands of crucified, consecrated men. Soft-living self-pamperers have no influence. Lives poured out as a glad thank-offering to God shame and attract a selfish world. Livingstone poured out his life for Africa as few men have ever done and then said, "People talk about the sacrifices I have made in spending so much of my life in Africa. . . . I never made a sacrifice." He regarded his exhausting labors and self-denial as a small part of the love debt he owed to God. So the burnt offering was accompanied by a song of joy.

When the body of Livingstone was buried in Westminster Abbey, the satirical humorous magazine, *Punch*, published the following lines,

" 'Tis the last mile of many thousands trod
  With failing strength but never-failing will,
By worn frame, now at its rest with God,
  That never rested from its fight with ill.

Or if the ache of travel and of toil
  Would sometimes wring a short, sharp cry of pain
From agony of fever, blain and boil,
  'Twas but to crush it down and on again!

———————

Open the Abbey doors and bear him in
  To sleep with king and statesman, chief and sage,
The missionary come of weaver kin,
  But great by work that brooks no lower wage.

He needs no epitaph to guard a name
  Which men shall prize while worthy work is known;
He lived and died for good—be that his fame;
  Let marble crumble: this is Living-stone."

Three weeks after Livingstone's funeral came the anniversary of the Church Missionary Society. In the Abbey service, Gordon Lathrop preached a remarkable sermon before a congregation actually seated over the new-made grave of Livingstone—and his text was the striking narrative of the dead body that came alive when it was cast into the sepulchre of Elisha and touched the prophet's bones. Among other things, the preacher said "Let us be quickened into fresh life by contact with the bones of Livingstone! and let thousands of Africans, through the influence of his death, be revived and stand up on their feet."

135

We are challenged and quickened by the lingering influence of some dead men who yet speak, while some living men who are dead leave us cold. Those who bear the cross of Christ will ever wear the crown of royal power.

Few things have moved me more deeply through the years than a tribute that appeared in *The Free Methodist* long ago, written by a young man in memory of an uncle who was well known in the church. This young man had never embraced the faith of his fathers. Part of the tribute reads thus, "One keenly realized that the man was mourned and remembered because of his work. His fellow workers were the important mourners; kinship was less than fellowship. This was reassuring to one who had seen men lost in a complicated civilization, achieving no individuality in their work. To a nephew, though, there was a deep pathos also. There was a man who had given unstintingly and sacrificingly to a cause. He symbolized his generation. Within a single family there was a generation that had done much toward the establishment and ramification of an institution. One thought of one's own generation in that family, its bewilderment, its helplessness, its impaired usefulness to the institution that was more than family to the older generation. The new generation—though thought of exceptions readily occurred—this new generation had been altered by the world, had become something different. . . . To be sure the institution was not without its second generation; one's father and cousins' fathers had been fathers in Israel, too. Sorrow was not for the institution (though there were questions about even its new generation), but one's self and one's contemporaries—a generation in danger of missing what was cherished as essential by the parents and of trying to carry

136

on without the heritage that the parent generation considered greatest.

"One could only hope that the recognition would lead to some assurance. It was plain that a man had lived a life of good work, that his church was paying him honor, that his fellow workers were singing 'Good-night' expecting to say 'Good-morning.' What a nephew thought or felt was of little importance when he had not shared in the work. So he realized, yet he saw in it something of wonder and admiration. He thought that it was necessary to recognize the parent generation's great and good ideal, and he hoped that his own generation might somehow prove worthy."

In this tribute which embodies a poignant confession you have a picture of one who admired the ideal and turned away from it sorrowful as did the rich young ruler in the Gospels. If the heritage is offered by those who loved not their lives to the death to preserve it, men may refuse it but they will be haunted by the memory of its attractiveness. Many will accept it and many who for a time despise and reject it will return at last to seize it.

"For Humanity sweeps onward, where today the martyr stands,

On the morrow crouches Judas with the silver in his hands;

Far in front the cross stands ready and the crackling faggots burn,

While the hooting mob of yesterday in silent awe return

To glean up the scattered ashes into History's golden urn."—James Russell Lowell

137

A life sacrifice will challenge and charm the men of the world, where a lip service only will leave them unaffected.

May God give us grace to handle our heritage as a trust and transmit it undiminished and untarnished to those who are to follow, so the old man's dream may become the young man's vision from generation to generation.

If the Elijahs of the older generation live close to God, when they depart the young Elishas will not be satisfied with a mantle of method to hold as an heirloom. They will cry for a double portion of the spirit that rested upon the departed, and they will go forth in the spirit and power of Elijah to perpetuate a holy religion and project its influence into the generation that follows them. So shall the Church of Christ continue to be a praise in the earth from age to age.

This book is set in 10 point Electra type and printed letterpress on West Virginia Book paper.

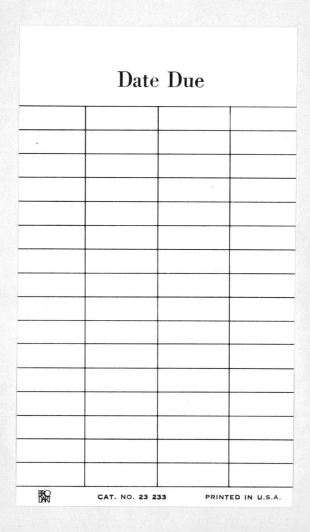

Date Due

BRODART   CAT. NO. 23 233   PRINTED IN U.S.A.